CORRECT,

NOT

POLITICALLY CORRECT

About Same-Sex Marriage and Transgenderism

EXPANDED THIRD EDITION

AWARD-WINNING AUTHOR
FRANK TUREK

Correct, Not Politically Correct:
About Same-Sex Marriage and Transgenderism
Expanded Third Edition
By Frank Turek

Sixth printing, 2024

CrossExamined.org
PO Box 78956
Charlotte, NC 28271

www.CrossExamined.org

Distributed by MorningStar Publications, Inc.,
a division of MorningStar Fellowship Church
375 Star Light Drive, Fort Mill, SC 29715

www.MorningStarMinistries.org
1-800-542-0278

Cover & Layout: Rebecca Lambertsen

ISBN: 978-1-60708-707-6

TABLE OF CONTENTS

ABOUT THIS THIRD EDITION OF *Correct, Not Politically Correct*

This third edition is divided into three sections written between 2008 and 2023.

The first section (Parts I-IV) was published in 2008. This section is the original book which makes a natural law/ public health case against same-sex marriage. This led to me being fired from two Fortune 500 companies. (I've learned that people fighting for "inclusion, tolerance, and diversity" will exclude and not tolerate you for holding a diverse view no matter how reasonable or nice you are about it.) I have not changed anything in that section for three reasons.

First, the arguments have not changed. I think they still constitute good reasons to be for natural marriage and to oppose making marriage genderless by mandating same-sex marriage. Second, you can judge for yourself if the thoughts I express in the original version, and how I express them, should disqualify someone from working in corporate America. Third, the original predictions are sadly coming true with each passing day.

The second section (Part V) was published in 2016. This section responds to new developments, especially the United States Supreme Court case *Obergefell v. Hodges*, which mandated same-sex marriage in every state in the union. That decision was to marriage what *Roe v. Wade* was to abortion. It took power away from citizens to govern themselves and imposed the opinion of five lawyers on 330 million people. While well intended, the decision makes marriage genderless, which will have negative effects on children and society moving forward.

The negative effects on children and society may take a generation to fully witness, but the losses of basic freedoms—freedom of conscience, speech, and religion—are now seen everywhere. Christians are losing their jobs and being fined for their religious or moral beliefs (I say "Christians" because LGBTQ activists rarely target Muslims). In this second section, I tell the story of how I lost my job, how others are losing their jobs, and why genderless marriage is a long-term problem.

The third section (Part VI) was published in 2023. This section addresses transgenderism, its meteoric rise, and why the arguments for gender transitioning do not work. People are being misled and hurt by the transgender craze. The most alarming aspects of this issue are the attempts to transition children—and in some states without parental consent. The Biden administration is even threatening to take children away from parents who refuse to transition their kids. I wish this were not the case, yet it is! We will see how politics have completely taken over sound science and medicine on this issue.

Now some might ask, "Why even discuss politics on these issues? Haven't Americans bought into same-sex marriage and transgenderism? What's the point?"

Same-sex marriage has wide support now, largely because the Supreme Court mandate has made people think, if it's legal, it must be moral (see "The law is a great teacher" in section one). However, transgenderism is a political-minority position, and parents are only beginning to wake up to its dangers.

Besides, politics is only one of at least two reasons we should stay informed on these issues. Yes, we want to influence our fellow citizens to pass good laws, but we also want to influence our friends and relatives to make good choices. Even if you don't have an opportunity to change laws, you have a decent chance of changing minds or informing your friends and loved ones. Even if you can't protect our country, you can help protect people in your life from making bad choices personally.

And who knows what will happen politically in the future? For nearly fifty years, pro-lifers were frustrated by the fact that *Roe v. Wade* stopped most pro-life legislation. Few thought it would ever happen, but now that case has been rightfully overturned (like marriage, abortion isn't in the Constitution). Conservatives living in red states can now save thousands of lives. One report showed that the number of abortions dropped 99% in Texas after the June 2022 Dobbs decision saved an estimated 50,000 lives![1]

---

1 Jon Brown, "Abortions in Texas plummet nearly 99% months after Dobbs ruling," *Fox News* (January 15, 2023).

Even if you think the chances of a significant political victory are remote, that shouldn't diminish your commitment. If you are a Christian or someone else who is concerned about children and the health of our nation, our job is to be faithful. We should fight for truth whether assured of political success or not. We must do what is right and leave the results to God. If we truly love people (including those who oppose us), we will do what is right, even if it costs us personally. When we exhibit the courage to do what is right, we embolden others to do the same.

How can we do that? This book is intended to help.

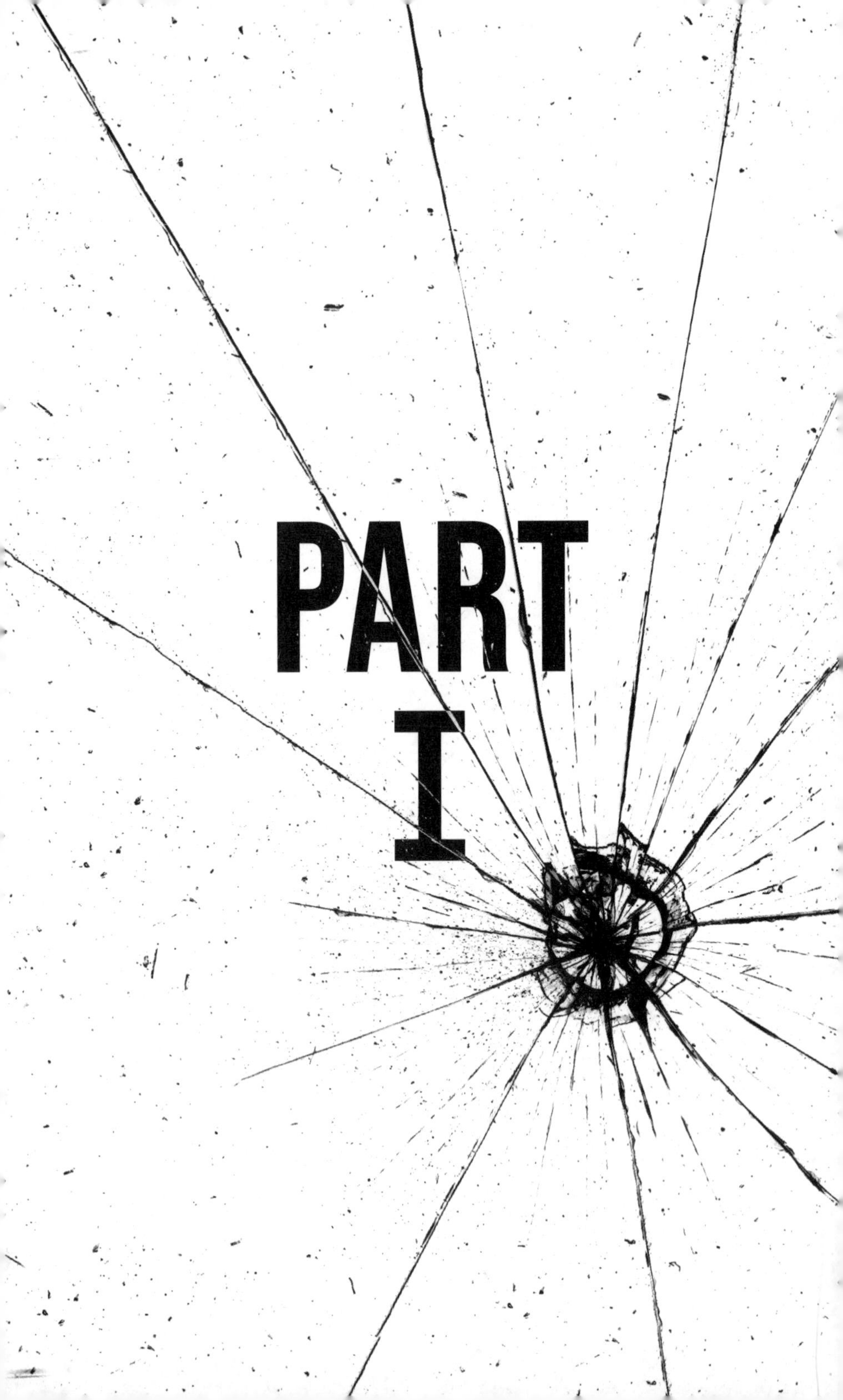

PART I

Introduction: Beyond Tolerance

Why do you care if homosexuals marry one another?

I wish I could say that same-sex marriage is okay (I only get abuse by opposing it), but I can't.

Why not? Same-sex marriage wouldn't hurt you!

Actually, it would hurt everyone—me, you, children, our country, and even homosexuals.

How so?

I'll tell you why, but you need to know something first.

What's that?

It's not my intention to be politically correct, just correct.

You're not going to be offensive, are you?

Not deliberately. But I've found that some people find the truth offensive.

That's fine. I can take it.

All right, here we go.

What should you do if someone close to you tells you he's gay? Cry? Shrug? Rejoice?

We are coming to the point culturally that if we don't respond with anything less than joy and celebration, we are unenlightened homophobes who need therapy. We are told that gay people are born that way, so it's better to accept that person for who he is rather than forcing him to live a lie.

A childhood friend of mine told his parents that he was gay. First, there was shock and denial, but soon there was acceptance and even approval. About fifteen years later, we buried my friend at the age of thirty-six—dead from AIDS.

Could his family have prevented this? I don't know, but in my opinion the approach they took didn't help. After my friend announced that he was acting on his homosexual feelings, his parents, who were wonderful, loving people, made a well-intentioned but tragic mistake. In their noble effort to love their son, they failed to distinguish between their son and the behavior of their son. They rightfully accepted him as a person deserving of love, but they failed to raise any objection to the behavior that would ultimately lead to his death.

Love requires us to stand in opposition to behavior that will likely hurt or kill our loved ones. In other words, it is unloving to enable or endorse destructive behavior. Regardless of where homosexual feelings come from (feelings are not a choice but behavior certainly is), it is unloving to pretend that there is nothing wrong with behavior that often results in such tragic outcomes. In fact, in today's society we've stood common sense on its head. We are not asked just to be tolerant anymore—we are now called bigoted homophobes if we don't endorse the demonstratively false assertion that homosexual sex and marriage are just as healthy and moral as heterosexual sex and marriage.

I think we need to stand against this harmful tide of political correctness. We need to tactfully expose the bad arguments and fallacious slogans offered in support of homosexuality and same-sex marriage. We need to point out that endorsing those things is not loving but actually hurts everyone, including homosexuals. That's what I will attempt to show in this book.

Before anyone accuses me of "gay-bashing," please allow me to state my intentions directly. This book is not meant to disparage anyone, including people who consider themselves gay. This book is simply meant to express disagreement over a public policy question. Just like I disagree with many of my heterosexual friends over certain issues, I also disagree with my friends who advocate homosexuality and same-sex marriage, whether they consider themselves gay or straight.

Any book that addresses the political question of same-sex marriage cannot avoid the issue of homosexual behavior. However, the focus of this book is *not* about the morality or immorality of homosexuality or same-sex marriage (although we will touch on that). The focus of this book is about whether either of those things should be endorsed and promoted by the government. I will argue that even if you think that there is nothing morally wrong with homosexual behavior, there are very good reasons why you should oppose same-sex marriage. In this book I will attempt to show why the evidence supports that position.

If the evidence actually does support that position, does it mean everyone will adopt that position? Of course not. Good arguments will not convince anyone who is not open to being convinced. We can all ignore facts that contradict our desires because desires will overrule the mind when we want them to. This is especially true in issues involving sex. As one of the most powerful forces in human nature, the unchecked sex drive can cloud good reasoning and even foster disdain for those trying to be reasonable about it. So I doubt that there is any evidence that I, or anyone, could offer to convince those who are determined to stay on the other side of this issue.

However, if you are someone who is open to truth, I hope this book will help you to stand for that truth personally and politically. As we are about to see, there is nothing gay about the long-term effects of government-backed same-sex marriage. The negative effects will be extremely damaging to this country and its citizens. That's why we all need to set emotion aside and act according to the facts. The first fact we need to realize is that this debate is not what most people think it is about.

What the Same-Sex Marriage Debate is Not About

In 1988, a group of prominent homosexuals got together in Warrentown, Virginia, to map out their plan to get homosexuality accepted by the general public. In the book that resulted from their meeting, they revealed a strategy that achieves its effect "without reference to facts, logic or proof... the person's beliefs can be altered whether he is conscious of the attack or not."[2]

In other words, their strategy was pure propaganda. That propaganda campaign has many people today believing that denying same-sex marriage involves denying rights to a victimized minority. That belief could not be further from the truth. In fact, let me suggest what the same-sex marriage debate is *not* about.

- It is not about equality or equal rights.
- It is not about discrimination against a class of people.
- It is not about denying homosexuals the ability to commit to one another.
- It is not about love or private relationships.
- It is not about tolerance or intolerance.
- It is not about bigotry or homophobia.
- It is not about sexual orientation or being born a certain way.
- It is not about race or the civil rights struggle.
- It is not about interracial marriage.
- It is not about heterosexuals and divorce.
- It is not about the separation of church and state.
- It is not even about religion.

"But that's all I hear about," you say. Of course, that's because the propaganda campaign continues to be successful. Those topics are all smoke screens designed to divert you.

2 The book was by Marshall Kirk and Hunter Madsen, *After the Ball: How America Will Conquer Its Fear and Hatred of Gays in the 90s* (New York: Penguin, 1989), pgs. 152-153.

In fact, for homosexuals, this debate isn't even about marriage. As data from countries with same-sex marriage show, *approximately 96 percent of homosexuals don't get married when they are given the opportunity.*[3] And those who do get married break up at a much higher rate than heterosexuals.[4]

So What Is the Debate About?

Since most homosexuals don't want to get married or stay married, then why are homosexual activists so adamant about government recognition of same-sex marriage? *Because same-sex marriage will win them what they really want—validation and normalization.* In other words, the activists want same-sex marriage because they understand that government-backed same-sex marriage will validate and normalize homosexuality throughout society.

The key point here is "government-backed." Homosexuals can already "marry" one another privately. There is just no government provision for it. Nothing is stopping homosexuals from pledging themselves to one another in private

---

3 In the Netherlands, which has had same-sex marriage since 2001, only between 2 and 6 percent of homosexuals have married. Such low numbers are consistent in other areas as well (we'll use the average of 4 percent or 96 percent who have not married). The rate is highest at 16.7 percent in the early days of same-sex marriage in Massachusetts. But that number, which is still low, is probably reflecting the same pent-up demand found in the Netherlands where the number of same-sex marriages has declined every year since 2001. See Maggie Gallagher and Joshua Baker, "Demand for Same-Sex Marriage: Evidence from the United States, Canada, and Europe," Institute for Marriage and Public Policy, April 26, 2006. Posted online at http://www.marriagedebate.com.

4 The "divorce" rate for homosexual men in Norway and Sweden is 50 percent higher (1.50) than heterosexual marriage, and the lesbian divorce rate is more than 150 percent higher (2.67). See Gunnar Andersson et al., "The Demographics of Same-Sex Marriage in Norway and Sweden," *Demography* 43, 2006: 79-98. For a number of articles containing research on homosexuality see www.americansfortruth.com.

same-sex marriage ceremonies. In fact, it is done all the time—there is an entire cottage industry for gay weddings.

But that's not enough for homosexual activists. What they want is government endorsement for their relationships. They know that such endorsement will make homosexuality and their behavior appear just as normal as heterosexuality. That's why the same-sex marriage movement has more to do with respect than rights.

Greg Koukl puts this very well: "Same-sex marriage is not about civil rights. It is about validation and social respect. It is a radical attempt at civil engineering using government muscle to strong-arm the people into accommodating a lifestyle many find deeply offensive, contrary to nature, socially destructive, and morally repugnant."[5] Same-sex marriage advocate Andrew Sullivan understands this. He writes, "Including homosexuals within marriage would be a means of conferring the highest form of social approval imaginable."[6]

This is the *real* reason homosexual activists are relentlessly pushing to get the government to endorse same-sex marriage. Most don't want to get "married," but they do want the social approval that same-sex marriage will win them.

At the end of the day, this debate is about only one question—*how far will we allow the courts to go to make homosexual behavior appear no different than heterosexuality?* I say the courts because the push for same-sex marriage is

---

5 Greg Koukl, "Same-Sex Marriage—Challenges and Responses, " May 2004, posted online at www.strradio.org.

6 Quoted in Greg Koukl, "Same-Sex Marriage—Challenges and Responses," May 2004, posted online at www.strradio.org.

not a movement of the people—it is a movement against the people. Homosexual activists don't want the people to vote on same-sex marriage because they know, in most states, they will lose. They continually file lawsuits in order to get the courts to take the issue away from the people as was done with abortion. That way same-sex marriage can be imposed on the people without their approval. You can't vote on it. You just have to accept what a few unelected judges say about it.

The United States Supreme Court has already struck down state anti-sodomy laws, but that's not enough for homosexual activists. They don't want mere tolerance. They want the state to go beyond tolerating homosexual behavior to endorsing it by changing the legal definition of marriage.

So far their strategy is working. Four members of the California Supreme Court overturned the votes of more than four million Californians to mandate same-sex marriage there. If that ruling stands, same-sex marriage laws could ultimately be imposed across the country. (True to form, homosexual activists filed a lawsuit in 2008 to keep Californians from voting to overturn the court decision.) If you have no moral objection to homosexual behavior or same-sex marriage, you might say, "Why not? Why shouldn't we endorse it?"

Here is the short answer: *By endorsing same-sex marriage, we will be sacrificing our children, our health, and our prosperity.* This will not happen immediately, of course, but over the long-term. In fact, even if you consider yourself "pro-homosexual," I hope you will see that the damage same-sex marriage will do to our children, our health, and our prosperity is not worth any perceived benefit to homosexuals. In fact, I will argue that same-sex marriage would actually hurt homosexuals.

The Six-Point Case Against Same-Sex Marriage

I'm sure you have several questions and objections to what I've just said. I hope I can answer them in the ensuing pages. Of course, I cannot make my complete case on page one, so I beg your patience. The following points are the case I will attempt to make:

1. Natural marriage is *the* foundation of a civilized society.
2. Homosexual behavior is inherently destructive.
3. The law is a great teacher, and it encourages or discourages behavior.
4. Government-backed same-sex marriage would encourage and normalize homosexual behavior, and it would harm natural marriage, children, adults, and homosexuals themselves.
5. The law should promote behaviors that are beneficial and prohibit (or at least not endorse) those that are destructive.
6. Therefore, the law should promote natural marriage, and it should provide no option for government-backed same-sex marriage or civil unions.

Obviously, these points need to be supported with evidence. I will take each one of them in order, and then answer the arguments for same-sex marriage and address the smoke screens I mentioned earlier.

For those of you who just want the bottom line, there is an executive summary at the end of this book. However, please do not rely exclusively on the executive summary. It's there to help you clarify and remember the basic arguments, but it's not a substitute for the main part of the book. Same-sex marriage is a complicated issue, the truth of which is sometimes difficult to communicate in sound bites. Some arguments did not make it to the executive summary, and all of the supporting data is in the main body of the book which is short. Due to the immense implications of this topic, I hope you will read it all.

the elderly. The United States' birth rate is about 2.1 per couple—any lower and the nation cannot sustain itself without immigration.

Children from natural marriage homes are:

a. Seven times less likely to live in poverty[10]
b. Six times less likely to commit suicide[11]
c. Less than half as likely to commit crime[12]
d. Less than half as likely to become pregnant out of wedlock[13]
e. Develop better academically and socially[14]
f. Healthier physically and emotionally when they reach adulthood[15]

These positive results of marriage are not new to our twenty-first century culture. Since virtually the dawn of humanity, marriage has been the bedrock of human social structure. In fact, British anthropologist J.D. Unwin studied eighty-six civilized and uncivilized cultures spanning five thousand years and found that the most prosperous cultures were those that maintained a strong marriage ethic. Every civilization that abandoned this ethic, including the Roman, Babylonian, and Sumerian empires, experienced demise soon after liberalizing their sexual practices.[16] A

---

10 See Patrick F. Fagan et al., "The Positive Effects of Marriage: A Book of Charts," The Heritage Foundation, http://www.heritage.org/research/features/marriage/index.cfm.

11 Michael J. McManus, "Why Is It in the Government's Interest to Save Marriages?" The Heritage Foundation, http://www.heritage.org/research/family/WM80.cfm.

12 Ibid, Fagan, Chart 17.

13 Ibid, Fagan, Chart 29.

14 Ibid, Fagan, Chart 21.

15 Ibid, Fagan, Charts 16-29.

16 Joseph Daniel Unwin, *Sex and Culture* (London: Oxford University Press, 1934).

civilized and productive society will not long endure if its adults abandon their children and one another in order to pursue sexual desires outside of natural marriage.

Imagine a society where increasing numbers of individuals have no stable family and must therefore fend for themselves. Without the natural family—which provides people with their most basic needs—social chaos will soon follow. In fact, virtually every social problem we have can be traced back to a problem with the family. If you don't think so, just take a look at the cost of broken homes to America.

If we restate the findings listed above in a different way, we can better comprehend the impact of fatherlessness.

First, children from fatherless homes are:

a. Seven times more likely to live in poverty
b. Six times more likely to commit suicide
c. More than twice as likely to commit crime
d. More than twice as likely to become pregnant out of wedlock
e. Worse off academically and socially
f. Worse off physically and emotionally when they reach adulthood

Second, children from fatherless homes account for:

a. 60 percent of America's rapists
b. 63 percent of America's youth suicides
c. 70 percent of America's long-term prison inmates
d. 70 percent of America's reform school attendees
e. 71 percent of America's teenage pregnancies

f. 71 percent of America's high school dropouts
g. 72 percent of America's adolescent murderers
h. 85 percent of America's youth prisoners
i. 85 percent of America's youth with behavioral disorders
j. 90 percent of America's runaways[17]

One problem with same-sex marriage is that it would increase the number of children without fathers. We'll see how later.

The importance of marriage is further evident when one considers that men and women can do almost everything alone—we can eat, breathe, think, move, etc. without anyone else. The singular exception is procreation. The sexes need one another to procreate. That should tell us that men and women were intended to procreate and parent together. In fact, without the procreative union of a man and a woman (and forgive me for stating the obvious), no one would exist, including homosexuals. Procreation alone should tell us about the supreme importance of marriage.

Some will say, "But some marriages do not produce children." Yes, but we are not talking about the singular exceptions, we are talking about marriage as an institution. While some marriages don't produce children, those that do are the building blocks of civilization. If there is any institution that's designed for the good of children and society, it is natural marriage. In other words, marriage of a man and a woman is fundamentally about the production and good of children and the civilization of society. That holds true

17 Most of these fatherless statistics, with references to their original sources, can be found here: http://fathersforlife.org/divorce/chldrndiv.htm.

even if some individual marriages don't do so. All books are designed for reading, even if some of them are never read.

Is it possible for children to thrive in homes without their biological moms and dads? Of course, that's just the exception rather than the rule. Family structure is the most important factor in a child's development. A loving mom and dad clearly provide the best structure. More than ten thousand studies show the significant advantages that children experience when raised by committed and loving moms and dads.[18] Unfortunately, homosexual relationships always deny children either their moms or their dads.

Homosexual activists claim, without any evidence, that parents are interchangeable—that two men or two women can do just as good a job in parenting as a man and woman because men and women offer nothing unique to children.[19]

This raises the following question for those making such an absurd and unsupported assertion: Why do you think that men and women are interchangeable as parents but not as sex partners? I mean, if men and women are really interchangeable, then why not just marry someone of the opposite sex?

Think about the inconsistency here. When it comes to their own personal gratification, homosexual activists clearly recognize the big difference between the sexes. Only when it

---

18 Dr. James Dobson, *Marriage Under Fire*, (Sisters, Oregon, Multnomah), 2004, pg. 54.

19 Even pro-homosexual researchers admit that homosexual parenting studies are flawed because political views often bias the findings. Contrary to what some studies supposedly found, the sexual behavior of the parents *does* affect children. See Kelley O. Beaucar, "Homosexual Parenting Studies are Flawed, Report Says," July 18, 2001. http://www.foxnews.com/story/0,2933,29901,00.html. For a personal testimony of someone who grew up in a homosexual household and staunchly opposes it, see Dawn Stefanowicz's book *Out from Under: The Impact of Homosexual Parenting,* (Annotation Press, 2007). You can read her moving testimony at http://www.dawnstefanowicz.com.

The benefits of natural marriage cannot be overstated. It benefits the married couple, their children, our economy, and the nation as a whole. In fact, natural marriage serves as a kind of national immune system. When our marriages are strong, our nation is strong and our social problems are few. When our marriages are weak, so is our nation.

Natural marriage:

a. **Lengthens life spans** of men and women.[7]
b. **Civilizes men** and focuses them on productive pursuits. Unmarried men cause society much more trouble than married men. (How many married men do you know who rove neighborhoods in street gangs?)
c. **Protects women,** who often give up or postpone their careers to have children, from being abandoned and harmed economically by uncommitted men.
d. **Protects mothers** from violent crime. Mothers who have never been married are more than twice as likely to suffer from violent crime as mothers who have married.[8]
e. **Lowers welfare costs** to society.[9]
f. **Encourages an adequate replacement birth rate,** resulting in enough productive young people to contribute to society and provide social security to

---

7 See *Marital status and longevity in the United States population*, http://www.ncbi.nlm.nih.gov/pubmed/16905719. For those not married, having never been married is the strongest predictor of premature mortality.

8 Robert E. Rector, Patrick F. Fagan, and Kirk A. Johnson, "Marriage: Still the Safest Place for Women and Children," The Heritage Foundation, www.heritage.org/research/family/bg1732.cfm.

9 Patrick F. Fagan et al., "The Positive Effects of Marriage: A Book of Charts," The Heritage Foundation, http://www.heritage.org/research/features/marriage/index.cfm. Charts 7-8.

The Six-Point Case Against Same-Sex Marriage

1. **Natural marriage is *the* foundation of a civilized society.**

Same-sex marriage activists want to define marriage as simply a private relationship between two, loving, committed parties. Sounds reasonable. If I had homosexual desires and decided to act on them, I might want the same thing.

However, marriage is much more than the private relationship of two people in a marriage. Marriage is a social institution that provides society with the very foundation of civilization—the procreating family unit. There would be no stability for children and, therefore, no community without marriage. In fact, marriage is the oldest and most basic of the three foundational institutions of Western civilization (the other two are government and the church). It is the most basic of the three because without children there would be no need for a government or a church, and no government or church can parent like a mom and a dad.

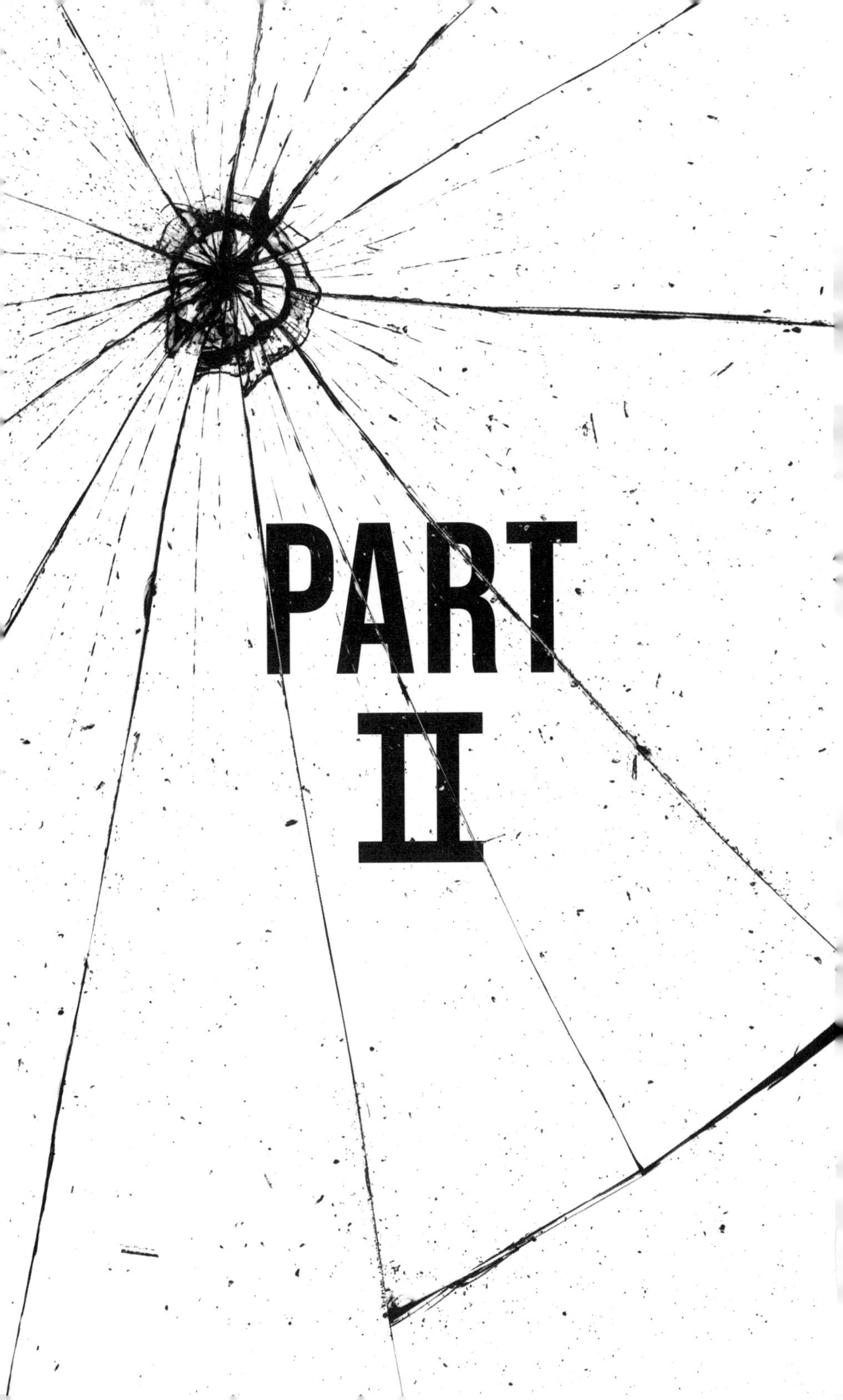

PART II

comes to the more important priority of raising children do homosexual activists say there is no difference between the sexes. Children are just going to have to take a backseat to homosexual sexual desires. Dr. Jennifer Roback Morse sums up the attitude of homosexual activists well. She writes, "[Homosexual] adults are entitled to have what they want. Children have to take what we give them."[20]

People who deny what's best for kids in order to have the sex they want show that they do not have the best interests of children in mind. This is another reason why homosexual relationships should never be equated to marriage. Marriage means much more than just sexual coupling as all children know.

When we sum this all up, we see that natural marriage: produces children, cares best for children, protects and enhances the lives of adults, and stabilizes society. Doesn't it make sense to protect it?

As we'll see in point 3, keeping marriage solely between a man and a woman will help protect natural marriage and children. But first, we need to take a candid look at the effects of homosexual behavior.

2. Homosexual behavior is inherently destructive.

This point often sends homosexual activists into a rage. They want so badly for homosexual behavior to be the equal of heterosexual behavior that they will deny the evidence and attack the character of the researchers who report about

---

20 Dr. Jennifer Roback Morse, *Marriage and society and the boundaries of gay adoption,* posted online at http://www.jennifer-roback-morse.com/articles/gay_adoption.html.

the negative health effects of the gay lifestyle. Despite their objections, there is valid data to show that male homosexuality in particular is extremely unhealthy.

Before we look at that data, I need to make clear that this point is not necessary for the case against same-sex marriage. In other words, even if homosexual activity was just as healthy as sex between a man and a woman, same-sex marriage should still be opposed because of the negative effects it would have on natural marriage and children, as we'll see later. I include this point only because it answers the claim that same-sex marriage would improve the health of homosexuals. It will not improve their health but probably hurt it. So let's get started.

It has been said that everyone is entitled to their own opinions but not their own facts. Unfortunately, homosexual activists act as if they are entitled to their own facts, one of which asserts that there is no real difference between heterosexual and homosexual relationships. Same-sex marriage advocate Andrew Sullivan writes, "[Gay marriage] says for the first time that gay relationships are not better or worse than straight relationships...."[21]

Sullivan is right—that's what government-backed gay marriage would say to the world—but that's exactly why we should not endorse it. The idea that "gay relationships are not better or worse than straight relationships" is utter nonsense. How can he deny that man-woman unions are the foundation of civilization? Doesn't he realize that he

21 Andrew Sullivan, "Here Comes the Groom: A Conservative Case for Gay Marriage," posted online at http://www.andrewsullivan.com/homosexuality.php.

would not exist or have grown up in such a civilized society without natural marriage?

The truth is that some relationships are better than others. People are equal, but their behaviors are not. Since homosexual behavior is contrary to the natural design and compatibility of the body, same-sex relationships can never function like man-woman relationships, nor can they birth the same benefits. So let's stop trying to equate same-sex with heterosexual relationships. They never can be the same. Biology prevents it and the evidence we are about to see disproves it.

Even if we ignore the issue of procreation, the evidence shows that homosexual unions are medically inferior to man-woman unions. Homosexual behavior:

a. Results in numerous health problems to those who practice it, including increases in AIDS, other STDs, colon and rectal cancer, and hepatitis. According to the Center for Disease Control, more than 82 percent of all known sexually-transmitted AIDS cases in 2006 were the result of male-to-male sexual contact. Moreover, gay and bisexual men account for more than 60 percent of all syphilis cases.[22]

22 The actual AIDS figure is probably higher than 82 percent because nearly all of the supposedly heterosexually-transmitted cases have a "risk factor not specified." Since homosexual contact is one of the most efficient ways of transmitting the disease, many of those not specified cases probably originated with homosexual contact. See Center for Disease Control, *Cases of HIV infection and AIDS in the United States and Dependent Areas, 2006 HIV/AIDS Surveillance Report*, Volume 17, April 2008. See Table 17: Reported AIDS cases, by age category, transmission category, and sex, 2006 and cumulative—United States and dependent areas. Available online at: http://www.cdc.gov/hiv/topics/surveillance/resources/reports/2006report/table17.htm. According to the Centers for Disease Control, gay and bisexual men account for the vast majority of syphilis cases (more than 60 percent in 2005). See also William Dunham, "Syphilis rise

b. Shortens the life span of homosexuals, probably by eight to twenty years (see note 22 for data on homosexual life span studies, some of which are controversial).[23] Smoking, on average, reduces life

---

in U.S. gay, bisexual men causes worry," Reuters, May 4, 2007. Posted online at http://today.reuters.com/news/articlenews.aspx?type=domesticNews&storyid=2007-05-04T170053Z_01_N04373052_RTRUKOC_0_US-SYPHILIS-USA.xml&src=rss&rpc=22.

23 John R. Diggs, Jr. M.D, *"The Health Risks of Gay Sex,"* Corporate Resource Council, 2002. Available on-line at http://www.corporateresourcecouncil.org/white_papers/Health_Risks.pdf. R.S. Hogg, S.A. Strathdee, K.J. Craib, M.V. O'Shaughnessy, J.S. Montaner, and M.T. Schechter "Modeling the impact of HIV disease on mortality in gay and bisexual men," *International Journal of Epidemiology, Vol 26,* 657-661. Available online at http://ije.oxfordjournals.org/cgi/content/abstract/26/3/657. Jeffrey Satinover, M.D., *Homosexuality and the Politics of Truth* (Grand Rapids, MI: Baker Books, 1996), 54, 69. For a recent study on HIV soaring among men having sex with teenage boys, see http://www.msnbc.msn.com/id/25398121.
More controversial studies have been conducted by Dr. Paul Cameron (http://www.familyresearchinst.org/). Some researchers and many homosexual activists question the methodology of Dr. Cameron's life span studies which found that the median age of death for male homosexuals is in the forties and lesbians in the fifties. A summary and discussion of Cameron's research can be found in "Only the gay die young? An exchange between Warren Throckmorton, Morten Frisch, Paul Cameron, and Kirk Cameron," August 2007, http://wthrockmorton.com/wp-content/uploads/2008/07/cameron.pdf. See also see Frank Turek and Norman Geisler, *Legislating Morality.* (Eugene, OR, Wipf & Stock, 2003), 259-260, (note 4).
The authors of the undisputed Hogg study, from which the 8-20 year life span reduction range comes, did not like the fact that some people were citing their study to oppose homosexual political goals. They issued a short "letter to the editor" four years after their initial study that concluded, "Overall, we do not condone the use of our research in a manner that restricts the political or human rights of gay and bisexual men or any other group." In the letter, they claim that deaths from HIV infections have dropped significantly in four years but gave no update to their 8-20 year figure (see http://ije.oxfordjournals.org/cgi/content/full/30/6/1499). Dr. Throckmorton in his exchange with Dr. Cameron (see reference above) made an admittedly "rough" speculation that the life span reduction is really three to seven years.
Some homosexual activists admit homosexuals die younger but blame "homophobia" for the reduction in life span. For example, in an overtly pro-gay piece, Christopher Banks from the University of Saskatchewan prepared a study for the Gay and Lesbian Health services in Saskatoon titled: *The Cost of Homophobia: Literature Review of the Economic Impact of Homophobia on Canada* (see http://www.lgbthealth.net/downloads/research/Human_Impact_of_Homophobia.pdf). Banks agrees with the numbers found in the study by Hogg, et. al. above, but says that homophobia drives homosexuals to drink more, smoke more, use drugs more, commit suicide more, etc.
This explanation, however, does not square with the facts. If "homophobia" was the cause of such health problems then we would expect such problems to disappear in societies that endorse homosexual behavior and marriage. That's not what we find at all. In places where homosexuality is widely accepted, even celebrated, the health problems are worse. Whatever the actual life span reduction is, this we know for certain: male homosexual contact in particular is inherently unhealthy, and encouraging it only leads to more health problems, not less. Encouraging homosexuality also leads to the other high-risk lifestyle choices that tend to go with it (smoking, drinking, drug use, etc.). Yet even if homosexual behavior were just as healthy as heterosexual behavior, same-sex marriage should still be opposed in order to protect children and the country.

span by seven years. Since we discourage smoking, why are we thinking of endorsing homosexuality?

c. Spreads disease to innocent people who never engage in homosexual sex. A prominent example is Ryan White, the teenage boy who died of AIDS after a blood transfusion. There are thousands of Ryan Whites—according to the CDC, there are nearly ten thousand known cases of innocent people in the United States who have contracted AIDS the same way, including 160 in 2005 and 131 in 2006 (this despite improvements in blood screening).[24] Moreover, there are thousands of innocent heterosexuals (many are spouses) who have contracted STDs via sexual contact with bisexuals.

d. Costs Americans millions in higher health insurance premiums because increased health costs from homosexual behavior are reflected in those premiums. In fact, the homosexual lobby has induced some states to prevent insurers from asking potential consumers any medical questions, including if they are HIV positive! As a result, every consumer is paying a higher premium because insurance companies are prevented from identifying clients who engage in high-risk sexual behavior.

The bottom line is that homosexual behavior is unhealthy. All sexual behaviors are not equally beneficial,

---

24 Center for Disease Control, *Cases of HIV infection and AIDS in the United States and Dependent Areas, 2005 HIV/AIDS Surveillance Report*, Volume 17, Revised Edition, June 2007. See Table 17: Reported AIDS cases, by age category, transmission category, and sex, 2005 and cumulative—United States and dependent areas. Available online at http://www.cdc.gov/hiv/topics/surveillance/resources/reports/2005report/table17.htm. See http://www.cdc.gov/hiv/topics/surveillance/resources/reports/2006report/table17.htm for 2006 numbers.

and some of them can have negative public consequences. Innocent people can and do get hurt.

Due to the devastating health effects of male homosexuality, most of the research into gay health issues has been concentrated on homosexual men. However, the research that has been conducted with respect to lesbians does not yield good news. Lesbians experience many more health problems than heterosexual women. Even the Gay and Lesbian Medical Association admits the following about lesbian women:

- Lesbians have the richest concentration of risk factors for breast cancer than any subset of women in the world.
- They have higher risks for cervical cancers.
- They are more likely to be obese.
- They use more tobacco, alcohol, and illicit drugs.[25]

A study of over 1,400 lesbians found the following:

- Lesbians experience higher rates of bacterial vaginosis and hepatitis C.
- They have more than twice the number of *male* partners than heterosexual women (only 7 percent who identify themselves as lesbians never have sex with men).
- They are 4.5 times more likely to have fifty or more male sexual partners in a lifetime.

25 Gay and Lesbian Medical Association, "Ten Things Lesbians Should Discuss With Their Health Care Provider," http://www.glma.org/index.cfm?fuseaction=Page.viewPage&pageID=691.

- They are three to four times more likely to have sex with men who are at high risk for HIV—homosexuals, bisexuals, and IV drug users.
- They are six times more likely to abuse drugs intravenously.[26]

Other studies also confirm lesbian health problems.[27]

Many homosexual activists get angry when you cite these health facts. But why would anyone get angry over facts? As Augustine said, we love the truth when it enlightens us, but we hate it when it convicts us.

However, other homosexual activists acknowledge negative health effects and then use them as a reason to support their cause. This "conservative" case for same-sex marriage suggests that homosexual monogamy, encouraged by government-backed same-sex marriage, would alleviate these health problems. Andrew Sullivan writes, "A law institutionalizing gay marriage would merely reinforce a healthy social trend. It would also, in the wake of AIDS, qualify as a genuine public health measure."[28]

Unfortunately, health problems and life span are not likely to improve significantly in so-called "committed" homosexual relationships. Why not?

---

26 Katherine Fethers, et al., "Sexually transmitted infections and risk behaviors in women who have sex with women," *Sexually Transmitted Infections* 76:345-349 (2000).

27 For a summary of lesbian health problems, see John R. Diggs, Jr. M.D, "The Health Risks of Gay Sex," *Corporate Resource Council*, 2002, pgs. 5-6. http://www.corporateresourcecouncil.org/white_papers/Health_Risks.pdf.

28 Ibid, Sullivan.

There are at least four reasons. First, monogamy is not the main issue—homosexual behavior is. Homosexual acts are inherently unhealthy, not just multiple-partner homosexual acts. This is especially true of male homosexuality. Does anyone really believe that it is natural and healthy to insert the penis into the rectum—the organ whose sole purpose is to expel poisons from the body? The rectum is a one-way street. It's a sewer. It was designed that way. Labeling its abuse as an act of "love" will not change that fact.

The standard homosexual response to this is, "It's natural for me because I desire to do it." I don't mean "natural" in the sense of desire, but "natural" in the sense of design. Human beings have all kinds of "natural" desires to do things that are physically destructive (e.g. smoking, getting drunk, violence, etc.), and those things often feel good. But we don't excuse those behaviors because they come "naturally." The human body was not designed for anal intercourse. Such an act violates the natural design, and having a desire to engage in it does not change the fact that it is unnatural and physically destructive.

Second, coupled homosexuals tend to practice more anal intercourse and more anal-oral sex than those without a steady partner. They also forego safer-sex practices because they are "in love."[29] In other words, coupled homosexuals tend to engage in more risky sexual contact than their single counterparts. So while married men improve their health and life span by being faithful to their wives, there is no comparable benefit in homosexual couples.

---

29 David Dunlap, "In Age of AIDS, Love and Hope Can Lead to Risk," *New York Times,* July 27, 1996.

Third, if AIDS will not break promiscuity in homosexuals, it is unlikely government-backed marriage will. As AIDS is falling among heterosexuals, it is rising among homosexual men.[30]

Finally, even if monogamy could reduce health problems, monogamy is the exception rather than the rule among homosexuals. The average number of sexual partners in a lifetime for a heterosexual is four, but for a homosexual it is fifty. The vast *Sex in America* survey published by the University of Chicago found monogamy among heterosexuals to be 83 percent but less than 2 percent for homosexuals.[31] Another survey had more moderate results, but still found infidelity in about 62 percent of gay couples. That led researchers in the *Journal of Family Psychology* to write, "The practice of sexual non-monogamy among some gay couples is one variable that differentiates gay and heterosexual couples."[32]

Why is monogamy much more common between men and women? Could it be because men and women are designed for one another and are therefore complementary? Think about it. One of the least-mentioned aspects of this debate is how men and women complement one another. Each sex balances and moderates the other by providing what's lacking in the other.

---

30 Mike Stobbe, "CDC understated number of new HIV infections in US," Reuters, August 2, 2008. http://news.yahoo.com/s/ap/20080802/ap_on_he_me/med_hiv_infections.

31 Jeffrey Satinover, M.D., *Homosexuality and the Politics of Truth* (Grand Rapids, MI: Baker Books, 1996), 54. The data from which Dr. Satinover draws these figures is the *Sex in America* survey published by researchers from the University of Chicago in 1994.

32 Quoted in Warren Throckmorton, Ph.D., "Chris Matthews' Hard Sell: Pay attention to the common Assumptions about Gay Marriage," online at http://www.pfm.org/AM/Template.cfm?Section=Home&TEMPLATE=/CM/ContentDisplay.cfm&CONTENTID=13210.

However, in same-sex relationships, the pairing of identicals propels them to extremes not balance. Lesbians tend to push one another to emotional extremes as evidenced by the intense demands they often put on one another, but male homosexuals experience the most damaging effects of imbalance. Instead of the sex drive of the man being balanced by the emotional needs of the woman, male homosexuals reinforce and amplify the sex drive of one another. That's why their behavior often becomes compulsive to the point of explosive promiscuity—anywhere from 21-43 percent of homosexual men have several hundred sexual partners![33]

In the late 1970s, A.P. Bell and M.S. Weinberg, in their classic study of male and female homosexuality, found that 43 percent of white male homosexuals had sex with 500 or more partners, with 28 percent having 1,000 or more sex partners. In the late 1990s, a study of the sexual profiles of 2,583 older homosexuals published in *Journal of Sex Research*, found that only 2.7 percent claimed to have had sex with one partner only. The most common response, given by 21.6 percent of the respondents, was of having a 101 to 500 lifetime sex partners.[34]

Tragically, some of those partners are children. While male homosexuals comprise only 2–3 percent of the male population, they commit about one-third of all child molestation cases. That is, about one-third of all pedophile cases are homosexual in nature—man to boy.[35]

---

33 See Van de Ven, Paul,; Pamela Rodden, June Crawford, and Susan Kippax (1997). "A Comparative Demographic and Sexual Profile of Older Homosexually Active Men." *J. of Sex Research* Vol. 34, No. 4, 1997. For a bibliography and summary of studies, see Timothy J. Dailey, Ph. D., "The Negative Health Effects of Homosexuality," *Insight,* Issue No. 232. Available online at http://www.frc.org/get.cfm?i=IS01B1.

34 Ibid.

35 One study found the figure to be 36 percent. See Kurt Freund, et al., "Pedophilia and

Now when someone connects homosexuality to pedophilia, homosexual activists are quick to deny the connection. However, the denial is for publicity reasons. In gay and academic publications and at gay "pride" parades, both which are largely unfamiliar to the general public, the gay rights movement and the North American Man-Boy Love Association (NAMBLA) are working together. Homosexual publications make favorable references to pedophilia, and homosexual activists and NAMBLA both want the age of consent lowered. They have friends in high places too. As an ACLU attorney, Supreme Court Justice Ruth Bader Ginsburg once advocated lowering the age of consent to twelve! Current Speaker of the House, Nancy Pelosi, marched with a leading advocate of man-boy "love" in the 2001 San Francisco gay "pride" parade.[36] (Of course, there was not a peep about this from the mainstream media.)

While homosexual activists try to deny the connection to pedophilia, most admit that homosexuals tend to be extremely promiscuous. As we have seen, reducing promiscuity is a central part of Andrew Sullivan's argument for same-sex marriage. Yet despite making the claim that same-sex marriage could improve homosexual monogamy, Sullivan doesn't really believe that gay monogamy is possible. Instead, he claims that homosexuals "need"

Heterosexuality vs. Homosexuality," *Journal of Sex and Marital Therapy* 10 (1984): 197. Another study found the figure to be 25 percent. See Ray Blanchard, et al., "Fraternal Birth Order and Sexual Orientation in Pedophiles," *Archives of Sexual Behavior* 29 (2000): 464. Whatever the precise number is, it is widely agreed that sexual abuse of boys is underreported. For additional studies and data on this issue, see Timothy J. Dailey, Ph. D., "Homosexuality and Child Sexual Abuse", *Insight,* Issue No. 247. Available online at http://www.frc.org/get.cfm?i=IS02E3#edn22.

36 See Brent Bozell, "Democrats on Sex and Children," TownHall.com, October 11, 2006, available online at http://www.townhall.com/columnists/BrentBozellIII/2006/10/11/democrats_on_sex_and_children. For more on the connection between homosexuality and pedophilia see: *The Problem of Pedophilia,* National Association for Research & Therapy of Homosexuality, September 21, 2004, available online at http://www.narth.com/docs/pedophNEW.html.

multiple partners! According to Sullivan (and just about every survey), monogamy is not "flexible" enough for homosexuals. He calls monogamy a "stifling model of heterosexual normality" and thinks homosexuals have a greater "understanding for the need for extramarital outlets."

But that's not the worst of it. Incredibly, Sullivan believes *heterosexuals* could learn from the promiscuity of homosexuals. He writes "something of the gay relationship's necessary honesty, its flexibility, and its equality could undoubtedly help strengthen and inform many heterosexual bonds."[37] In other words, instead of gays becoming more like straights, Sullivan thinks straights should become more like gays.

As we'll see later, this is what homosexual activists are really after—they don't want same-sex marriage so they can live in monogamy like most heterosexuals do—they want to tear down the standards of normalcy to the level of their own behavior. Only then will they feel validated.

In the meantime, let me point out that Sullivan is absurd to assert that the "flexibility" to engage in "extramarital outlets" could "strengthen" any marital bond, especially of a husband and wife. Certainly the last thing any family or our nation needs is for more married men and women to avail themselves of "extramarital outlets."

Sullivan's viewpoint on "extramarital outlets" is not surprising. It represents the strong strain of narcissism that runs through the homosexual movement and some homosexual relationships. From his perspective, homosexual

37 Andrew Sullivan, *Virtually Normal,* (USA: Vintage Books, 1996), pgs. 202-203.

relationships are all about self-gratification—they are about him and his desires. But a truly loving relationship isn't about the narcissistic desires of the individuals in it. Love, by definition, seeks the ultimate good of the loved one by "forsaking all others." It binds the lover to the loved one, not a nightclub full of anonymous partners.

Now, Sullivan is one of the most conservative advocates of same-sex marriage you will find. If Sullivan is for "extramarital outlets," imagine what the more radical advocates are for—the complete destruction of monogamy and natural marriage (quoted below). Actually, the "conservative" Sullivan is not far from that. By admitting that homosexuals "need" multiple partners, Sullivan is admitting that he wants to change marriage completely into something unrecognizable. Since his new definition cannot be about love, monogamy, or children, what will it be about?

Obviously, it will not be anything like natural marriage. The pairing of identicals, particularly in men, only feeds insatiable lust that leads to explosive promiscuity. But the natural balancing that takes place in a natural marriage is conducive to love, monogamy, and children. Anyone in natural marriage knows that a strong marriage requires the frequent sacrifice of your own comfort and desires for the good of your spouse and children. With loving sacrifice comes growth, maturity, and contentment. This is the polar opposite of the average homosexual relationship where you betray your family's trust, health, and well-being so you can indulge in the lust of an "extramarital outlet." Since this is the kind of relationship that homosexuals like Sullivan want to extol as "marriage," they need to call it something else.

The homosexual relationship they have in mind is closer to prostitution than natural marriage.

Yet even if homosexuals stopped their "extramarital outlets," and even if same-sex marriage could reduce some of the health problems of homosexuals, those unlikely possibilities do not justify making same-sex marriage the legal equivalent of natural marriage. The unique abilities to procreate and parent children should always keep natural marriage as the only legally and socially-encouraged sexual relationship in our society.

Why does the law matter? We'll see in point three.

3. The law is a great teacher, and it encourages or discourages behavior.

Homosexuals understandably want their relationships to have equal social status with those of heterosexuals, and they see the law as their weapon to force that acceptance on the public. Homosexual activist Michelangelo Signorile believes that same-sex marriage is "a chance to wholly transform the definition of family in American culture. It is the final tool with which to dismantle all sodomy statutes, get education about homosexuality and AIDS into public schools, and, in short, usher in a sea of change in how society views and treats us."[38]

Andrew Sullivan agrees. He writes, "If nothing else were done at all and gay marriage were legalized, 90 percent of the political work necessary to achieve gay and lesbian equality

38 Michelangelo Signorile, "I Do, I Do, I Do, I Do, I Do," *OUT Magazine*, May 1996, pg. 30.

will have been achieved. It's ultimately the only reform that matters."[39]

Now we've reached the real reason homosexual activists are fighting so hard for government-backed same-sex marriage. Their relentless push for same-sex marriage isn't really about civil rights—it's about civil acceptance. Government-backed same-sex marriage is the one law that will normalize homosexual behavior everywhere else.

Sullivan and Signorile are right about this. They recognize the power of the law to change behavior and attitudes over the long-run. The law is a great teacher—many people think that whatever is legal is moral and, therefore, should be accepted. We only need to look at two of the most divisive issues in the history of our country—slavery and abortion—to see the power of the law to influence attitudes and behavior.

At the onset of the Civil War, our country was basically split on the issue of slavery, but today virtually everybody believes that slavery is morally wrong. What changed? We certainly haven't become more religious or pious. No, what has changed is the law. The Thirteenth Amendment to the United States Constitution has helped teach each new generation that slavery is wrong.

Unfortunately, a change in the law can also lead new generations astray. When the Supreme Court issued its *Roe vs. Wade* opinion in 1973, most Americans thought abortion was wrong as evidenced by the laws in each of the fifty states

39 Andrew Sullivan, *Virtually Normal,* (USA, Vintage Books, 1996), pg. 185.

which outlawed or restricted it. But today, the country is about evenly split. What happened? The law changed. In a situation that is the reverse of slavery, what was once considered immoral (and thus illegal) suddenly became a right created by the federal government. Legalization led to more social acceptance of abortion and a sixteen-fold increase in abortions nationwide. If same-sex marriage receives government backing, we will likely see an increase in homosexual behavior as well.

A third example of the law's impact is divorce. Homosexual activists are right when they say that heterosexuals have degraded marriage through divorce. Given the negative impact of divorce on children and society, I think divorce laws should be tightened. Divorce should be an absolute last resort.

But the fact that heterosexuals have degraded marriage through divorce is *not* an argument for same-sex marriage. In fact, the recent history of the law and divorce actually argues *against* same-sex marriage. The vast social problems we are experiencing since the liberalization of divorce laws should help us realize just how important the law is to the health of the family and the country. When you pass laws that weaken the family, the entire nation gets sick. This should cause us to protect marriage, not weaken it further. When a patient has a disease, giving him another disease is not a prescription for wellness.

How would same-sex marriage hurt natural marriage? Point 4.

4. Government-backed same-sex marriage would encourage and normalize homosexual behavior, and it would harm natural marriage, children, adults, and homosexuals themselves.

How would same-sex marriage hurt natural marriage?

This may be news to many Americans, but some college professors and other liberal radicals can't stand natural marriage. They agree with the sentiments of the Gay Liberation Front which proclaimed back in 1969, "We expose the institution of marriage as one of the most insidious and basic sustainers of the system." To them, marriage is a hindrance to achieving full public acceptance of radical sexual liberty. That's why these people devote themselves to the complete destruction of the institution of marriage.

One of the leaders of this movement is Judith Stacey, the former Barbra Streisand Professor of Contemporary Gender Studies at the University of Southern California (I'm not making this up!). Stacey, who now teaches at New York University, declares, "I object to the profoundly discriminatory and antidemocratic character of the policies [marriage] promotes."[40] Stacey's disdain for marriage is so great that she actually applauds rising divorce rates!

Despite this, Stacey is actually one of the nation's staunchest supporters of same-sex marriage. *In fact, most people who professionally dislike marriage support*

40 Judith Stacey, "Letters", *The Nation*, October 1, 2001, posted online at http://www.americanvalues.org/html/page124951.html.

same-sex marriage.[41] Why is this so? Because Judith Stacey and her allies understand that the endorsement of same-sex marriage would spell the destruction of natural marriage. Stacey quotes law professor, Nan D. Hunter, who argues that government-backed same-sex marriage would have "enormous potential to destabilize the gendered definition of marriage for everyone."[42]

Michelangelo Signorile admits that is his strategy as a homosexual activist. His goal isn't to get government-backed same-sex marriage so he can adhere to marriage's moral code like straights do. (He can already do that without the government getting involved. And remember, just about every other homosexual is like Signorile—96 percent of them do not get married when given the chance.) His goal is to destroy marriage itself. He urges his fellow homosexual activists "to fight for same-sex marriage and its benefits and then, once granted, redefine the institution of marriage completely, to demand the right to marry, not as a way of adhering to society's moral codes but rather to debunk a myth and radically alter an archaic institution."

Sneaky? Subversive? Exactly. In fact, Signorile goes on to write, "The most subversive action lesbian and gay men can undertake . . . is to transform the notion of 'family' entirely.[43]

Paula Ettelbrick, former legal director of the Lambda Legal Defense and Education Fund, agrees. She admits,

41 David Blankenhorn, *The Future of Marriage*, (New York, Encounter Books), 2007, pg. 28.

42 Judith Stacey, *In the Name of the Family*, (Boston: Beacon Press, 1997), pgs. 123-124.

43 Michelangelo Signorile, "Bridal Wave," *Out*, December 1994. Quoted in Timothy J. Dailey, Ph. D., Homosexual Parenting: Placing Children at Risk, *Insight*, Issue No. 238. Available online at http://www.frc.org/get.cfm?i=IS01J3.

"Being queer is more than setting up house, sleeping with a person of the same gender, and seeking state approval for doing so . . . Being queer means pushing the parameters of sex and sexuality, and in the process transforming the very fabric of society."[44]

We need to realize what these homosexual and anti-family zealots realize. (Remember, these are the people who hate natural marriage but are for same-sex marriage.) They realize that changing the definition of marriage will destroy marriage itself because the new definition will help change the attitudes and behaviors of our citizens. By dragging natural marriage down to their level, marriage will be destroyed, and their sexual choices will be validated. They are correct!

If you are still not sure how changing the law would destroy marriage, consider an analogy. Right now, the legal benefits given to married couples affirm the fact that we consider natural marriage to be the most valuable sexual relationship in our society. That is, if sexual relationships were players on a sports team, marriage would get the most valuable player (MVP) award. In sports, that's an esteemed award because it's given only to the player whose performance is truly the most valuable. But suppose the league's commissioner redefined the qualifications required to win the MVP award to the point where everyone in the league received the award, even those who performed poorly. Would anyone think the MVP award was special? Obviously not—everyone would think it was meaningless! Who would even take the trouble to go pick it up? No one.

---

44 Quoted in Tim Leslie, "The Case Against Same-Sex Marriage," *Crisis,* January 8, 2004. Available online at http://www.crisismagazine.com/january2004/leslie.htm.

In the same way, the value of natural marriage will be diminished if we redefine the qualifications of marriage to include same-sex relationships and confer the same benefits on those relationships. We need to face the fact that just as all players are not equally valuable to a team, all relationships are not equally valuable to a society. Natural marriage is the most valuable relationship in any civilization. That's not bigotry—that's wisdom based on evidence from five thousand years of human experience, the self-evident design of the human body, and the documented beneficial results of natural marriage to children, their parents, and our society.

If we allow any other sexual relationship to have the same status as natural marriage—be it man-man, woman-woman, man-daughter (incest), man-woman-man, or whatever-whatever—we will degrade marriage itself (just like we degrade the MVP award by giving it to everyone). When we degrade marriage, we will get less of it. When we get less of it, we will further weaken our civilization. Children will be hurt the most.

How would same-sex marriage hurt children?

David Blankenhorn is the founder and president of the non-partisan Institute for American Values, an organization devoted to strengthening families and civil society. Blankenhorn describes himself as a lifelong, liberal Democrat[45] who disagrees with the Bible's prohibitions of homosexuality.[46] He also buys into the fallacious notion that people who have

45 David Blankenhorn, "Strengthening America's Families," "Letters", *The Nation,* October 1, 2001, posted online at http://www.americanvalues.org/html/page124951.html. See also David Blankenhorn, *The Future of Marriage*, (New York, Encounter Books), 2007, 302.

46 David Blankenhorn, *The Future of Marriage*, (New York, Encounter Books), 2007, pg. 210.

homosexual desires are somehow a special class of people who do not have equal rights.

Despite this, Blankenhorn makes a powerful case in his book, *The Future of Marriage*, that same-sex marriage must not be endorsed. He writes, "Here is my dilemma: With every fiber of my being, I want to affirm the equal dignity of all persons and push for equal treatment under the law. Yet I'm also a marriage nut. I've spent most of my professional life arguing that marriage is important and that children need mothers and fathers."[47] So while Blankenhorn sympathizes with homosexuals, he still believes that arguments against same-sex marriage far outweigh those for it.

Why? He cites some of the reasons I've given here, but the good of children is his most crucial reason. He observes, "Across history and cultures . . . marriage's single most fundamental idea is that every child needs a mother and a father. Changing marriage to accommodate same-sex couples would nullify this principle in culture and in law."[48]

How would same-sex marriage "nullify" parenthood and hurt children? The law is a great teacher: Once the government endorses the idea that marriage is just a legal contract between consenting adults of any gender (i.e. regardless of procreative realities), then marriage will no longer be seen as a prerequisite for children. Marriage will be seen as nothing more than coupling. In fact, that's exactly how Andrew

---

47 Ibid, pg. 128.

48 Ibid, pg. 178. Emphasis in original.

Sullivan sees marriage now. He writes that "coupling—not procreation—is what civil marriage now is."[49]

If government-backed same-sex marriage is legalized, "coupling" is exactly how future generations will see the institution of marriage. If that view prevails, many more couples in our society will forgo natural marriage and have more children out of wedlock. Why go through the trouble of getting married to have children if marriage isn't about children? Why tie yourself to one person if you don't need to?

This further erosion of marriage will hurt children because illegitimate parents (it's not the fault of the children) often never form a family, and those who cohabitate break up at a rate of two to three times that of married parents.[50] When illegitimacy rises, not only do children suffer, but the rest of us are forced to pay high social costs because of the resulting increases in crime, poverty, taxes, and social spending. (Recall from point 1 that children from broken homes, particularly fatherless homes, are responsible for a majority of violent crimes and youth problems.)

Are these just the hysterical warnings of an alarmist? No. We can look at results in other countries for confirmation. For example, in Norway, a country that has had de-facto same-sex marriage since the early nineties, illegitimacy is exploding. In Nordland, the most liberal county of Norway, where they fly gay "rainbow" flags over their churches,

49 Ibid, pg. 178. Emphasis in original. http://www.andrewsullivan.com/index.php?dish_inc=archives/ 2004_01_25_dish_archive.html#107526329968381529. Also quoted by Stanley Kurtz in "Slipping Toward Scandinavia," *The National Review*, February 2, 2004. http://www.nationalreview.com/kurtz/kurtz200402020917.asp.

50 Stanley Kurtz, "The End of Marriage in Scandinavia," *Weekly Standard*, February 2, 2004, http://www.weeklystandard.com/content/public/articles/000/000/003/660zypwj.asp.

illegitimacy has soared—more than 80 percent of women giving birth for the first time do so out of wedlock, and nearly 70 percent of all children are born out of wedlock. Across the entire country of Norway, illegitimacy rose from 39 percent to 50 percent in the first decade of same-sex marriage.[51]

Anthropologist Stanley Kurtz writes, "When we look at Nordland and Nord-Troendelag—the Vermont and Massachusetts of Norway—we are peering as far as we can into the future of marriage in a world where gay marriage is almost totally accepted. What we see is a place where marriage itself has almost totally disappeared."[52]

But it's not just Norway. Blankenhorn reports this same trend in other countries. International surveys show a mutually re-enforcing relationship between same-sex marriage and illegitimacy. Natural marriage is weakest and illegitimacy strongest wherever same-sex marriage is legal.[53]

You might say, "Correlation doesn't always indicate causation." Yes, but often it does. Is there any doubt that liberalizing marriage laws impacts society for the worse? You need look no further than the last forty years of no-fault

51 Stanley Kurtz, "The End of Marriage in Scandinavia," *Weekly Standard*, February 2, 2004, http://www.weeklystandard.com/content/public/articles/000/000/003/660zypwj.asp.

52 Kurtz, "Slipping Toward Scandinavia." Kurtz responds to his critics in, "Smoking Gun: The Netherlands shows the effect of Same-sex Marriage," in National Review Online, June 2, 2006. Available here: http://article.nationalreview.com/?q=MDFhMjk0YjI4NzgyZGM4NjMxZmY-4NTQwZWNjYzkzYjg.

53 For example, only 37 percent of people from countries with same-sex marriage think they should marry if they want children while 60 percent of people from countries *without* same-sex marriage think so. The same attitude holds true with regard to cohabitation: 83 percent think it's acceptable in same-sex marriage countries, but only 49 percent think so elsewhere. See David Blankenhorn, *The Future of Marriage*, (New York, Encounter Books), 2007, pg. 233.

divorce laws in the United States (family disintegration destroys lives and now costs tax payers $112 billion per year[54]).

No-fault divorce laws began in one state, California, and then spread to rest of the country. Those liberalized divorce laws helped change our attitudes and behaviors about the *permanence* of marriage. There is no question that liberalized marriage laws will help change our attitudes and behaviors about the *purpose* of marriage. The law is a great teacher, and if same-sex marriage advocates have their way, children will be expelled from the lesson on marriage.

Furthermore, homosexual activists are fighting to change marriage laws because they know that there is a causal connection between law and behavior. As people like Sullivan and Signorile have admitted, they don't want to change the law so they can get married, but because they know that a change in the law will change the attitudes and behaviors about marriage and homosexuality for all of society.

Blankenhorn and Kurtz also understand the causal connection between the law, attitudes, and behavior. That's why they argue so forcefully against same-sex marriage. Blankenhorn asserts that anyone concerned about the welfare of children cannot be a supporter of same-sex marriage. He writes, "One can believe in same-sex marriage. One can believe that every child deserves a mother and a father. One cannot believe both."[55] Why? Because, as data from other countries show, "redefining marriage to include

54 See the 2008 report titled "The Taxpayer Costs of Divorce and Unwed Childbearing" at http://www.marriagedebate.com/pdf/ec_div.pdf.

55 David Blankenhorn, *The Future of Marriage*, (New York, Encounter Books), 2007, pg. 201.

gay and lesbian couples would eliminate entirely in law, and weaken still further in culture, the basic idea of a mother and a father for every child."[56] Blankenhorn goes so far as to say that he is amazed at how indifferent gay activists are about the negative effects of same-sex marriage on children. Many of them, he documents, deny that marriage has anything to do with children.[57]

He goes on to warn that if same-sex marriage is adopted, the claim that "every child needs a father and a mother" will probably be viewed as "divisive and discriminatory, possibly even as hate speech."[58] He doesn't have to be much of a prophet to predict that. Canada and Sweden already restrict speech against homosexuality to the point that even pastors have been jailed for quoting Bible verses.[59] In the United States, the Democrat Party continually puts forth "hate-crime" legislation which will lead to the same result. Endorsement of same-sex marriage will only pave the way for the hate-crime thought-police to get here faster.

Regarding the situation in Scandinavia, Kurtz writes, "Instead of encouraging a society-wide return to marriage, Scandinavian gay marriage has driven home the message that marriage itself is outdated, and that virtually any family form, including out-of-wedlock parenthood, is acceptable."[60]

---

56 Ibid, pg. 3.

57 Ibid, pg. 152.

58 Ibid, pg. 3.

59 Harry Jackson Jr., "The Massacre of the Pulpit," April 23, 2007, posted on-line at http://www.townhall.com/Columnists/HarryRJacksonJr/2007/04/23/the_massacre_of_the_pulpit.

60 Kurtz, "The End of Marriage in Scandinavia."

Well, if marriage is not about children, what institution is about children? And if we are going to redefine marriage into mere coupling, then why should the state endorse same-sex marriage at all? Contrary to what homosexual activists assume, the state doesn't endorse marriage because people have feelings for one another. The state endorses marriage primarily because of what marriage does for children, and in turn, for society. Society gets no benefit by redefining marriage to include homosexual relationships, only harm, as the connection to illegitimacy shows. The very future of children and a civilized society depends on stable marriages between men and women. That's why, regardless of what you think about homosexuality, the two types of relationships should never be legally equated.

We have enough problems already with illegitimacy in America. We don't need to make matters worse. Unfortunately, if we go the route of other countries and approve government-backed same-sex marriage, we will likely get the same results—a significant rise in illegitimate parenthood and all of the social problems that come from it. Children will be hurt the most, but so will you.

How would same-sex marriage hurt you?

Homosexual activists ask, "How would government-backed same-sex marriage hurt you?" Most conservatives have failed to answer this question, but it is not hard to foresee the following negative consequences on all Americans:

1. **Income taxes will be increased** to make up for the marriage tax benefits given to homosexual couples

and to pay for the social costs resulting from the increase in illegitimacy. We provide financial benefits to married couples because they produce and care for children. Why should homosexual couples get the same benefits as men and women raising children? Moreover, providing financial incentives for homosexual unions would be doubly counterproductive. First, taxpayers would be subsidizing, and thus encouraging destructive behavior. Second, we then would pay for the results of that behavior in the form of increased medical and social costs.

2. **Social security taxes will be increased (or benefits decreased)** in order to pay survivor support benefits to homosexual "widows" and "widowers."

3. **Medical insurance premiums will rise** to offset the higher health care costs associated with homosexual behavior (i.e., AIDS, colon cancer, hepatitis and other diseases) which will likely increase if we approve same-sex marriage. Medical premiums would rise further if insurance companies are mandated to cover fertility treatments for lesbian couples (there's sure to be some judge somewhere to order that!).

4. **Employee benefits will be reduced** as employers are mandated to spread their limited benefit dollars to include homosexual partners. Limited benefit dollars given to homosexuals must come from somewhere; indeed, they are taken away from everyone else—married couples raising children.

5. **Homosexual couples will be given legal preference to adopt** due to their inability to procreate. In other words, homosexuals will not be granted equal rights but super rights—rights that will supersede your rights as a citizen. Tragically, children will be treated as trophies that, in effect, validate homosexual relationships.

6. **Your children will be indoctrinated,** with or without your consent, to accept homosexual behavior and same-sex marriage as the moral and social equivalent of heterosexual behavior and marriage (we are seeing this in our public schools already, especially in California and Massachusetts).

7. **Your workplace will attempt to indoctrinate you** to the same ends—and if you refuse, you will either lose your job or not be considered a "team player." (This is already happening through "diversity" training in many companies; it will become universal if same-sex marriage becomes law.)

8. **Your place of worship will be forced to hire homosexuals** and play by new draconian rules that impose homosexuality. A Catholic adoption charity recently closed its doors in Massachusetts rather than offer children to homosexual couples as the state mandated. This new rule was the direct result of government-backed same-sex marriage. Tolerance will become a one-way street—you need to tolerate and even advance homosexuality, but homosexual activists don't need to tolerate your views.

9. **Free speech and religion rights will be curtailed** as opposition to homosexuality is criminalized as "hate speech" (as is now the case in Canada and Sweden). This should wake up religious people who erroneously believe they ought not to be involved in politics. Politics affects your ability to practice your religion! Once same-sex marriage is approved, it will not be long before you will be fined or imprisoned for expressing any opposition to homosexuality. People with religious moral convictions will be considered worse than racists.

10. **Your government and its intrusive ways will grow** as a result of the changes we have just reviewed. That's another reason why liberals love same-sex marriage—it means more big government. They will call for more government programs to fix the mess caused by the destruction of the family and more government regulation to ensure that their new morality of political correctness is imposed on you, your children, and your place of worship.

These negative effects are indeed significant, but as we have seen, the most dramatic impact will come upon future generations. That's because same-sex marriage will change the way future generations think about homosexuality and marriage itself. Ironically, this would also hurt homosexuals.

How would same-sex marriage hurt homosexuals?

For more than two hundred years of our country's history, homosexual behavior was considered bad enough to prohibit as evidenced by the many state laws against sodomy. When the Supreme Court nullified those laws in the 2003 *Lawrence vs. Texas* decision, it sent a message that suddenly homosexual behavior was not bad enough to prohibit—now we must permit it.

That is a significant paradigm shift, but it's nothing compared to the complete reversal of thought that the imposition of same-sex marriage would represent. If the court or congress mandates same-sex marriage, it will be in effect saying that sodomy is now good enough to promote—from prohibit, to permit, to promote.

Same-sex marriage would promote the obviously false idea that homosexual behavior is just as healthy and beneficial as heterosexual behavior. This would not only hurt society, but it would hurt homosexuals as well. How so?

Given the serious health consequences of homosexual behavior, we would be unloving as a society to endorse it. We would not be merely allowing people to destroy themselves, but we would be encouraging them to do so.

David Kupelian writes this well in his book, *The Marketing of Evil*: "We've forgotten as a society what love is, because supporting and justifying homosexuality is not real love any more than glorifying drinking helps the alcoholic or celebrating smoking helps wipe out lung cancer . . . The most loving stance for others to take is not to serve as enablers of self-destructive and immoral compulsions, but to stand in patient but firm opposition."[61]

---

61 David Kupelian, *The Marketing of Evil,* (Nashville, WND Books, 2005), pg. 37.

Why don't we stand in patient but firm opposition? Because it's much easier to uncritically accept the half-truths put out by homosexual activists, and then have what seems to be compassion for them by giving them what they want. But that's not real compassion. Jay Budziszewski observes that real "compassion ought to make us visit the prisoner, dry out the alcoholic, help the pregnant girl prepare for the baby, and encourage the young homosexual to live chastely. But how much easier it is to forget the prisoner; give the drunk a drink, send the girl to the abortionist, and tell the kid to just give in. False compassion is a great deal less work than true."[62]

People are being hurt by our false compassion that promotes homosexuality. Such false compassion not only entices more young adults to experiment with homosexuality, but makes the struggle more difficult for homosexuals who would like to leave the lifestyle. As George Gilder points out, "Some gays . . . are not helped by the aggressive gay liberation movement that wants to flush them out of the closet and into the street where they can be exploited by the gay rights brigade. They want to live quietly and productively and are thoughtful enough not to want to inflict their problem on others."[63] Indeed, promoting problem behaviors is anything but compassionate.

Homosexual activists may object to the suggestion that we know what's best for them. "Keep your compassion to yourself. I want to behave this way!" they might say.

---

62 J. Budziszewski, *What We Can't Not Know*, (Dallas: Spence, 2003), pg. 190.

63 George Gilder, *Men and Marriage*, (Adler, 1986), pg. 74.

Well, you can behave that way, but don't expect the rest of society to endorse it. That would be unloving. Promoting homosexuality with government-backed same-sex marriage would not only hurt you, but it would also hurt our children and our country.

5. The law should promote behaviors that are beneficial and prohibit (or at least not endorse) those that are destructive.

Same-sex marriage activists want to define marriage as simply a private relationship between two, loving, committed parties. They think it's unfair that heterosexual relationships are recognized when their relationships are not. This is a misunderstanding of why the state is involved in marriage at all.

The state does not endorse natural marriage because two people "love" one another. It endorses man-woman unions because they benefit the public welfare in the numerous ways we've seen (children, health, reduced social costs, etc.). Besides, if marriage is merely a private affair, as same-sex advocates contend, then why do they want the government involved at all? They do not need the government to do what they want to do. As I mentioned above, people who have homosexual desires can pledge fidelity to one another already—they don't need state sanction to do so.

By their own admission, the main reason homosexuals want the government involved is to force acceptance of homosexuality on the public. I apologize for the repetition, but I cannot emphasize this enough. They want to change the law because they know that's the way to change cultural attitudes about their behavior. In other words, state sanction will lead to social sanction. The approval of the law will lead to approval of homosexuality. Since many activists consider homosexual behavior their identity, any approval of homosexuality means approval of them as people. That's what this is about. It's not really about marriage but the validation marriage will bring them.

But government doesn't exist to validate the desires of its citizens when such validation would harm others or society. To the contrary—the main purpose of government is to protect its citizens from harm. That's why good laws endorse behaviors that are beneficial to the public welfare and restrain behaviors that are destructive to it.

James Madison, the father of our Constitution, put it well. He wrote, "If men were angels no government would be necessary." Since we're not angels, government's role is to discourage harm and encourage good. No society can long endure when its government reverses that duty.

6. Therefore, the law should promote natural marriage, and it should provide no option for government-backed same-sex marriage or civil unions.

I have argued that natural marriage is beneficial while same-sex marriage would be destructive. If you are still not convinced, consider this: What would be the effect on society if everyone lived faithfully in natural marriage? It would result in a dramatic reduction in crime, welfare, abortion, and child abuse. On the other hand, what would be the effects on society if everyone lived faithfully in same-sex marriage? It would be the end of society and the human race itself. While universal homosexuality, of course, would not occur, the two questions should help us realize that the two types of relationships can never be equated because they are not equally beneficial.

Simply put, homosexuality is not good for individuals or societies. And while governments cannot feasibly prohibit all negative behaviors, they certainly can avoid promoting those that are. At the very least, our government must avoid promoting homosexual behavior and same-sex marriage.

Marriage is hard enough as it is in our over-sexualized culture. The media advertises instant gratification and mocks the ideals of natural marriage, making it more difficult for couples to commit to one another or to stay together once they do. The last thing we need is for the law to encourage the same kind of destructive behavior as well.

The conclusion regarding same-sex marriage follows from the case we have seen here. But why not accept the compromised position of "civil unions?" Because civil unions would still give government endorsement and financial benefits to a destructive behavior. Language manipulation will not change that fact. Renaming a bad law will not alleviate the negative effects of that law.

PART III

Answering Arguments for Same-Sex Marriage

Homosexual activists have done a great job advancing their cause with slick moralistic slogans about equal rights, discrimination, and so forth. As we will see, few, if any, of the pro-same-sex marriage slogans tell the truth. They sound good to a passive audience, but upon closer analysis, they are exposed as half-truths and deceptive distortions.

The activists have been able to get away with that because our fast-paced lives and sound-bite media provide the perfect environment for propaganda to replace truth. It only takes ten seconds to utter a lie, but it can often take ten minutes to provide enough evidence to explode that lie. The problem for the truth is that there is no such thing as a ten-minute sound bite (that's why this is a book, not a slogan).

The questions below help expose the false premises behind arguments for same-sex marriage. Take a minute to marinate on each of these questions and consider how you would respond. If you are honest, I think that your common sense responses will help expose the fallacies hidden in most pro-same-sex marriage arguments:

1. Are all kinds of sexual contact the same? Is sexual contact ever unhealthy and/or unloving?
2. Are people ever born with conditions that are not normal and sometimes harmful?
3. Should the government promote harmful behavior?
4. Is there any difference between sexual desires (orientation) and sexual behavior?
5. Should people act on every desire they have?
6. Must the government recognize every desire people have as a right?
7. Is there a difference between skin color and sexual behavior?
8. Are children usually better off with a mom and a dad, or is parenting irrelevant to their development?
9. What's more beneficial to a society—endorsing homosexuality or endorsing good parenting?
10. Should the government endorse behavior that is usually harmful but in rare exceptions is not?
11. Is there a difference between religion and morality?
12. If marriage has been weakened by liberalized divorce laws, does it make sense to weaken it further by liberalized marriage laws?
13. What would be the effect on society if everyone lived faithfully in natural marriage?
14. What would be the effect on society if everyone lived faithfully in same-sex marriage?

Now that you have considered these questions, let's look at each pro-same-sex marriage argument specifically. We'll see how these questions apply as we proceed.

We want equal rights!

Key Questions:

- Must the government recognize every desire people have as a right?
- Don't current marriage rules apply equally to everyone?

Answer: This is the main battle cry of homosexual activists. It's brilliant because who can be against equal rights?

The problem with the slogan is that, when it comes to marriage, everyone in America already has equal rights. We are all playing by the same rules—we all have the same right to marry any qualified person from the opposite sex. Those rules do not deny anyone "equal protection of the laws" because the qualifications to enter a marriage apply equally to everyone—every male and female has the same right to marry.

What certain males and females in our society want is special rights—the special right to marry someone of the same sex. But if we grant special rights for same-sex couples to marry one another, on what grounds can we deny special rights for consenting adults who desire marriage for other socially destructive or unhealthy relationships such as polygamy, incest, or bestiality? Should bisexuals get to marry two people?

You say, "We won't allow polygamy, incest, and bestiality because those are unhealthy and destructive relationships!"

Yes, but so are homosexual relationships as we saw in point 2 of the six-point case.

Second, as I have already mentioned, the government is not denying the "rights" of homosexuals to have relationships or to pledge themselves to one another "till death do them part." Homosexuals do that all the time. But homosexuals have no "right" to have that relationship endorsed and granted benefits by the state. Government endorsement is the central issue in this debate.

Third, desires do not constitute rights. Just because you have a desire to do something doesn't mean you have a right to do it. Even among "consenting adults," there is no right to prostitution, polygamy, adultery, or incest. And even if you were to claim a private right to such behavior, you certainly have no right to government endorsement of that behavior. Yet that's what homosexual activists demand for homosexuality.

Fourth, while proponents of same-sex marriage cast this as a moral issue (that's why they use the word "rights"), they lack any moral authority for their position. By whose standard of morality must same-sex marriage be established? Certainly no founding Constitution of any state, or the federal government, says anything about same-sex marriage. Is there a standard beyond the Constitution? Yes, God—but God is the last subject homosexual activists want to bring up. If they appeal to "nature's God"—or the "self-evident" "laws of nature" that come from God as the Declaration of Independence declares—then they have to make the case that God believes homosexual behavior and same-sex marriage is a right. That's anything but self-evident, as virtually the entire history of religion, the "laws of nature," and the design of the human body attest.

Finally, notice that homosexual activists cleverly avoid the real issue. When speaking of homosexuality, they always talk about rights rather than acts. They know they won't win if they describe the acts that they want us to endorse through government-backed same-sex marriage. Since a majority of Americans find such acts unnatural, immoral, and repulsive, homosexual activists hide the real truth about what they do behind the word "rights" because no one can be against that. This language manipulation extends to other terms they use (such as "gay" and "pride") and is a common propaganda technique used by radical abortion rights proponents as well. It's too difficult to advocate child dismemberment, so partial-birth abortion advocates talk about "choice." We should ask the manipulators the following: "A right to choose what?" and "A right to do what?" They won't call it what it is because the naked truth would hurt their case with most Americans.

Homosexuality is like race. Homosexuals are a class of people like African-Americans.

Key Questions:

- Is there a difference between skin color and sexual behavior?
- Why should we classify people because of what they desire to do sexually?

Answer: Homosexuals want to be considered a class of people by depicting themselves as victims who, like blacks, have been denied civil rights. That way, they can make the unsuspecting public think that those who oppose their political agenda arc discriminating against them rather than their behavior. According to them, conservatives are all bigots on par with racists—we are opposed to fairness itself.

But all of that is nonsense. First, the comparison of homosexuality to race is completely invalid. Skin color is benign, but sexual behavior is not. Having a certain skin color does not hurt anyone, but homosexual behavior can and does hurt others. Furthermore, *sexual behavior is always a choice; race never is*. You will find many former homosexuals, but you will never find a former African-American.

Second, homosexuality is not an identity or class; it's a behavior. Homosexuals are not a class of people any more than heterosexuals are a class of people. We are males and females, not gays and straights. In other words, we are males and females by anatomy, but gays and straights by behavior.

Why not classify people by their desires as homosexual activists demand? Because if we start to classify people by what they desire to do sexually, then why not give people with all sexual desires special marriage rights? On what grounds should we say that same-sex marriage is fine but not marriage involving polygamy, incest, or bestiality?

"But those behaviors are harmful!" you say.

Exactly, and so is homosexual behavior. So why is it legitimate to carve out a special case for homosexuality but not for those other behaviors?

Skin color and sexual desires do have one thing in common—they are both non-issues when it comes to law. Why should the law care about your skin color or desires of any kind? Laws should be concerned only with behavior.

People can desire to marry whoever or whatever they want, but the behavior of actually marrying a person is what the law is concerned with. As we've seen in the six-point case, the state has a compelling interest to keep laws that promote natural marriage and provide no option for government-backed same-sex marriage.

Homosexuals Were Born that Way!

Key Questions:

- Are people ever born with conditions that are not normal and sometimes harmful?
- Is there any difference between sexual desires ("orientation") and sexual behavior?
- Should people act on every desire they have?
- Homosexuals are born as males or females, so why should they follow their desires but not the design of their bodies?

Answer: Some homosexuals insist that they have had homosexual desires as long as they can remember. Somehow this is supposed to prove that these desires are the result of nature not nurture. But this argument ultimately fails to justify homosexual behavior or any behavior for that matter.

First, notice that "born-that-way" is an argument from nature or design: "Since I was designed with these desires,

I ought to act on them." The people who say this normally presume that the Designer is God.[64] But if you insist that God designed your desires, then you cannot deny He designed your body as well.

This raises the question to homosexuals who make this argument: *Why are you following your desires but not your body? After all, we're not sure if God designed your desires, but we are certain that He designed your anatomy. Why not follow what you know is from God?* Ignoring your desires can be uncomfortable, but ignoring the natural design of your body can be fatal.

We are not sure about a genetic source for homosexual desires because after many years of intense research, a genetic component to homosexual desires has not been discovered. We know genetics cannot explain homosexual desires completely. If they did we would expect identical twins to have the same desires, but twins do not. In fact, it's doubtful that genetics explains anything about homosexual desires. How would a homosexual "gene" be passed on? Homosexuals don't pass on anything because they don't reproduce.

Instead of nature, one's nurture (a person's childhood and environment) appears to have a more identifiable impact on homosexual desires. Several studies have shown that male homosexuals are more likely to come from families with a dominant mother and weak or distant father. Homosexuals are also more likely to have been sexually abused as

64 If atheism is true and random evolutionary processes got you to this point, you are under no obligation to live in any way. There are no "oughts" if there is no God. See footnote 66 for more.

children.[65] While the nature versus nurture debate will continue, it's probably impossible to identify all of the factors that go into a person's desires, sexual or otherwise.

But let's suppose that scientists someday discover a genetic contribution to homosexual desires. Would that give license to behavior? No, all of us have desires that we ought not to act on. In other words, we were all born with an "orientation" to bad behavior, but desires don't justify the behavior. For example, some may have a genetic predisposition to alcohol, but who would advocate alcoholism? If someone has a genetic attraction to children, does that justify pedophilia? What homosexual activist would say that a genetic predisposition to violence justifies gay-bashing? (Born gay? What if the gay-basher was born mean?). Desires do not justify behaviors. In fact, there is a word we use to describe the disciplined restraint of destructive desires—it's called "civilization."

Let me ask you this: Should human beings act on every desire they have? For the sake of civilization, are there any desires people ought not to act on?

For any civilization to survive, quite a lot of restraint is necessary. Unfortunately, homosexual activists will have none of this. Instead of restraining negative behaviors, homosexual activists are asking us not just to tolerate but to endorse them. They want laws that will encourage people with certain desires to engage in harmful behavior. That's exactly what the government should discourage, not promote.

---

65 For a summary of these studies, see Peter Sprigg and Timothy Dailey, co-editors, *Getting it Straight: What the Research Shows about Homosexuality,* (Family Research Council, Washington, D.C. 2004), pgs. 1-34.

Weren't you born a heterosexual?

Answer: No, I was born a male. What I decide to do sexually is a choice.

Actually, when we use terms like "gay" or "straight," we make it seem like people are in one class or the other. But such language is misleading. Nobody was born a heterosexual or homosexual—we were born males or females. For convenience, we use those terms when it would be more accurate to say "people who engage in heterosexual acts" or "people who engage in homosexual acts." In other words, we are males and females by biology, and heterosexuals or homosexuals by behavior.[66]

Now if you were to ask me, "Were you born with heterosexual desires?" I would say, "I don't know, but how could anyone know that?" How would you know for sure if your feelings are the result of nature or nurture or some combination? It's certainly possible that there's some kind of genetic component to heterosexual sexual desires. Since we are clearly designed to propagate, and since the vast majority of people have heterosexual desires, they would seem to be part of our normal design.[67]

---

66 Hermaphrodites (those born with male and female sex organs) are extremely rare among humans. The condition is considered a birth defect, and thus does not affect our line of reasoning here. Defects in design do not suggest how those without defects should behave. Moreover, hermaphrodites often choose one gender or the other, and some have surgery in doing so.

67 Design explains human beings better than random evolutionary processes. Moreover, since homosexuals don't reproduce, "natural selection" would have selected them to extinction by now if homosexuality had a genetic source. For the numerous problems with Darwinism and the evidence for design, see chapters 5 and 6 of my book, *I Don't Have Enough Faith to Be an Atheist,* co-authored with Norman Geisler, (Wheaton, Crossway, 2004).

However, we all know that in this imperfect world, a small percentage of people are born with conditions or characteristics that we would not consider natural or normal. Genes sometimes have defects. For example, some people are born deaf, blind, or with psychological and mental limitations or deficiencies. There is even evidence that some desires or personality traits—including anger, which can lead to the harmful behavior of violence—may have a genetic source. Other people may not be born with such traits or conditions but develop them during childhood.

Now here's the key point: *Whether such traits or conditions are the result of nature or nurture makes little difference—we all regard them as deficiencies. What we never do is pretend that such deficiencies are normal or encourage the harmful behavior that may flow from them.* For example, we never say that a defect in a man's sexual preference that predisposes him to pedophilia is normal, nor do we encourage him to follow those desires because of that defect.

Yet that's exactly what homosexual activists want us to do by endorsing same-sex marriage. They want us to pretend that homosexual desires and behaviors are normal. Again, they don't want us just to tolerate homosexual behavior—they want us to endorse it. It's bad enough to pretend that abnormal conditions are really normal and that harmful behaviors are not really harmful, but it's simply unconscionable to endorse harmful outcomes.

Why do they want endorsement? Again, because endorsement brings validation. They know the best way to achieve the complete validation of homosexuality throughout society is to have the government endorse same-sex marriage.

Homosexuals cannot change.

Answer: Cannot change what—behavior or orientation? Many homosexuals have changed not only their behavior but also their orientation (desires).

Thousands of ex-homosexuals testify of their change, and renowned Columbia University psychiatrist, Dr. Robert Spitzer, documented some of those changes. His 2003 study shows that some highly motivated individuals can change their orientation from homosexual to heterosexual through reorientation therapy.[68] This is significant because Spitzer is no propagandist for the religious right. Quite the contrary—a self-described "Jewish atheist," Spitzer was considered a hero by gay activists for getting homosexuality declassified as a mental disorder back in 1973. Homosexual activists don't like his new study though.

In an interview, Dr. Spitzer said that his study "has been criticized severely by many people, particularly gay activists, who apparently feel quite threatened by it. They have the feeling that in order to get their civil rights, it's helpful to them if they can present the view that once you're a homosexual you can never change."

When asked whether the American Psychiatric Association should now change their position statements that say orientation cannot be changed, Dr. Spitzer said, "I think they should, [but] they will not be . . . There's a gay activist

68 See Dr. Robert L. Spitzer, *Archives of Sexual Behavior,* Vol. 32, No. 5, October 2003, pp. 403-417. For a summary of the findings see Roy Waller and Linda A. Nicolosi, *Spitzer Study Published: Evidence Found for Effectiveness of Reorientation Therapy,* National Association for Research & Therapy of Homosexuality, September 21, 2004, available online at http://www.narth.com/docs/evidencefound.html.

group that's very strong and very vocal and is recognized officially by the American Psychiatric Association. There's nobody to give the other viewpoint. There may be a few who believe it, but they won't talk."

Dr. Spitzer then acknowledged explicitly that politics often trump the scientific facts at organizations like the APA.[69] He also said that the APA should stop applying a double standard by discouraging reorientation therapy, while actively encouraging gay-affirmative therapy that's intended to confirm and solidify a gay identity.[70] Good point by Dr. Spitzer. After all, if people can be talked into it, then why can't they be talked out of it?

But let's suppose that some homosexuals cannot change their orientation. Does that mean they cannot control their behavior? Why do we expect pedophiles to resist their desires but not homosexuals? Because we know pedophiles are human beings who can choose not to act on their sexual desires just like anyone else. We also demand them to resist their desires because our children will not be safe if they don't. As we've seen, our children will not be safe either if we endorse homosexuality because that endorsement will help destroy natural marriage.

The truth is, sexual behavior is not compulsory. It is always a choice. We all must resist our sexual urges at times. And while it's not desirable, some do so for their entire lives and never have sex. That's possible for people with any sexual

69 See Warren Throckmorton, PhD., "My interview with Dr. Robert Spitzer," posted online at http://www.drthrockmorton.com/interviewdrspitzer.pdf.

70 See Roy Waller and Linda A. Nicolosi, *Spitzer Study Published: Evidence Found for Effectiveness of Reorientation Therapy,* National Association for Research & Therapy of Homosexuality, September 21, 2004, available online at http://www.narth.com/docs/evidencefound.html.

desire. After all, if I honestly believe that I've been born with heterosexual desires, am I required to engage in heterosexual acts? Am I not capable of controlling my sexual desires and remaining celibate? If you claim that I am not, then you have also made the absurd contention that no one in the history of the world has ever been morally responsible for any sexual crime, including rape, incest, and child molestation.

Same-sex marriage is about love. Who could be against that?

Key Questions:

- What is the primary reason the state endorses marriage?
- Are all kinds of sexual contact the same? Is sexual contact ever unhealthy and/or unloving?
- What is "loving" about medically-destructive sexual contact?

Answer: You can't evaluate whether same-sex marriage is a good idea or not unless you know why the government endorses marriage in the first place. It is impossible to judge the means unless you know the intended ends.

So what is the government's main purpose for endorsing marriage? What ends are they trying to accomplish? Contrary to what homosexual activists assume, the government does not endorse marriage because two people love one another. There is no little box on a marriage license that you must check labeled "in love." In fact, many, if not a majority, of marriages around the world are arranged.

While it is true that we often associate marriage with love, the primary reason the government endorses marriage is because it brings the country as a whole tremendous benefits—it is the best way to produce children and propagate a civilized and stable society. Homosexual unions by nature cannot do that, and equating the two types of relationships diminishes the connection people make between marriage and childbearing.

Yet even if love is seen as a reason for marriage, we must ask, "What kind of love typifies a homosexual relationship?" Are there men who really feel drawn romantically to other men? No doubt. Are there men who really have a deep sense of commitment to other men, wish to care for them, and be intimate with them? No doubt.

But the same might be said of a man and his daughter, a man and a child, or three men and a woman. Should those people act on their sexual desires? If they did, would their actions truly be seeking the ultimate good of the person or persons they were trying to "love?" No. Sometimes sexual acts can be unloving. In fact, even sexual acts inside of natural marriage can be unloving—when they are medically dangerous for example. This is the case with homosexual acts. They are medically dangerous. What is loving about sex acts that regularly cause bleeding, disease, and pain? When sex is medically dangerous, the most loving thing you can do is not to have sex with that person.

Some may argue, "When two adults consent to engage in homosexual acts, they are each seeking the good of the other. Each person wants it and chooses it." But if you truly love someone, will you do something that is likely to cause disease and may even shorten their life span dramatically? As we saw in point 3, the life span of gay men may be as much as twenty years shorter than that for heterosexuals.[71] With the consequences so severe, if a man really "loved" another man, he wouldn't engage in homosexual acts with him. Besides, sex isn't the only way you can demonstrate your love for someone. Men usually demonstrate their love for one another without having sex. In fact, most of our loving relationships are non-sexual.

Yet even if homosexual relationships were just as healthy as heterosexual relationships, there is a big difference between permitting such relationships and promoting them. The government already permits homosexual relationships. They even permit private same-sex marriages—there is nothing stopping homosexuals from pledging lifelong fidelity to one another. But most states do not promote and provide benefits for such unions by offering government-endorsed same-sex marriage. And why should they? Homosexual relationships, no matter how much they are about love, cannot produce the same positive effects for the nation as heterosexual marriages. That's why, regardless of what you think about homosexuality, the two types of relationships should never be equated.

Some animals engage in homosexual behavior.

Answer: This "animals-do-it" argument is seriously put forth by homosexual activists. Yes, some animals engage in homosexual behavior on occasion, but some animals eat their young too. Should we do that as well?

---

71 See note 22.

When homosexual activists extol animals as their moral examples, what does that say about their own behavior? They are looking down when they should be looking up.

Opposition to same-sex marriage is like opposition to interracial marriage.

Answer: No, race is irrelevant to marriage—gender is essential to it. Nothing is wrong with interracial marriages because men and women are designed for one another, regardless of their racial backgrounds. But same-sex marriage is harmful because the human body was simply not designed for same sex relations. As we've seen, homosexuals pay a high physical price for contradicting that design. So our marriage laws should be color blind but not gender blind.

Furthermore, interracial marriage was opposed without any valid grounds. Opponents hid their prejudice with false speculation about birth defects and the like. Since all racial groups interbreed, such problems do not exist. In other words, there really is no such thing as interracial marriage because there is only one race—the human race. Interethnic marriage poses no physical problems. However, same-sex couples don't breed at all, and their unions are often unhealthy.

Ironically, it's not conservatives, but same-sex marriage proponents who are reasoning like racists. Instead of asking the state to *recognize* the preexisting institution of marriage, homosexuals are asking the state to *define* marriage. Well, that is exactly the line of reasoning racists used in their effort to prevent interracial marriage. Racists wanted the state to define marriage as only between same-race couples, instead of having the state recognize what marriage already was—the procreative union of a man and a woman regardless of their racial/ethnic background.[72] While racists and homosexuals may want to alter the legal definition of marriage, they cannot alter the laws of nature that helped produce the recognition of legal marriage in the first place.

Opposing same-sex marriage is bigotry.

Answer: Opposition to same-sex marriage is not based on bigotry but on good reason. Consider murder, rape, and incest. Our laws rightly discriminate against those behaviors because those behaviors are harmful. Imagine murderers, rapists, or the incestuous calling us "bigots" for enacting those laws. Such laws are the antithesis of bigotry. Bigotry involves pre-judging something for no good reason, but laws against murder, rape, and incest are based on good reason and evidence. Namely, we reasonably conclude that the health and welfare of the public are higher values than allowing individuals to do whatever they want.

The same holds true with preserving marriage. The health and welfare of the public are higher values than allowing individuals to marry whomever they want. We don't discriminate in favor of natural marriage and against same-sex marriage out of bigotry or bias, but because we are sensible human beings who draw on thousands of years of evidence to conclude that one sexual relationship is more beneficial than any other. Some behaviors are better than others. That's not bigotry; it's wisdom.

72 Thanks to my friend Dr. Francis Beckwith for this insight. See www.FrancisBeckwith.com for several fine articles dealing with social issues.

Of course, some proponents of same-sex marriage may continue to call us bigots, which could be considered evidence that their case is flawed. Since they cannot win on the merits, their only recourse is to divert attention through name-calling.

By the way, the bigotry charge is another case of selective morality on the part of homosexual activists. While resistance to same-sex marriage is clearly not bigotry as they claim, we might ask them, "Why is bigotry wrong? From what moral standard are you arguing? Why can you recognize that bigotry is absolutely wrong, but refuse to admit that homosexual behavior is wrong as well?" Indeed, homosexuals acknowledge nature's law when it comes to the immorality of bigotry, but they conveniently ignore it when it comes to their own homosexual behavior.

You are just a homophobe!

Answer: When people resort to name-calling, they have reached the end of their ability to articulate a rational argument. Nevertheless, there is a kernel of truth to it. Some people do have phobias, but some phobias are justified. Many people, for example, share a phobia of snakes, but that's because snakes can hurt you.

The fear that parents and loved ones have of homosexuality is not unjustified either. It has little to do with bigotry, ignorance, or a lack of understanding. Rather, it has everything to do with a complete understanding of the facts. In light of the documented dangers of homosexual behavior, family and friends have every reason to fear their loved ones getting involved in homosexuality. The health dangers, social dysfunctions, and inability to procreate are conditions no sane parent wants any child to choose.

Likewise, the fear that a majority of Americans have over same-sex marriage has a solid rational basis as well. It's based on the evidence, not prejudice.

I know loving homosexual couples with children who have been together for years.

Key Questions:

- Are children usually better off with a mom and a dad or is parenting irrelevant to their development?
- What is more beneficial to a society—endorsing homosexuality or endorsing good parenting?
- Should the government endorse behavior that is usually harmful, but in rare exceptions is not?

Answer: Family structure is the most important factor in a child's development. As we saw in point 1, having a mom and a dad is the best structure. Conversely, according to the American College of Pediatricians, the research shows that homosexual couples provide a far less safe and stable environment for children. They note that violence among homosexual partners is two to three times more common than among married heterosexual couples, and homosexual partnerships are significantly more prone to dissolution than heterosexual marriages, with the average homosexual relationship lasting only two to three years. Homosexuals are also more likely than heterosexuals to experience mental illness, substance abuse, suicidal tendencies, and shortened life spans. They conclude, "Given the current body of research, the American College of Pediatricians believes it is inappropriate, potentially hazardous to children, and dangerously irresponsible to change the age-old prohibition on homosexual parenting, whether by adoption, foster care, or by reproductive manipulation. This position is rooted in the best available science."[73]

Yet even if one could cite cases of homosexuals living long, healthy, monogamous lives and providing well for children, the research shows that such people are the exception rather than the rule, and laws must be based on what usually happens, not exceptions.

For example, we should not stop warning people about the dangers of smoking just because some smokers outlive non-smokers. Nor should we stop warning people about the dangers of homosexual behavior or parenting just because some homosexuals outlive heterosexuals or parent better. (If we're not going to warn them, at the very least, we ought not to endorse homosexual behavior through government-backed same-sex marriage.)

If laws were based on exceptions, we would have to do away with virtually every law we have. It would require that we do away with all laws against running red lights because sometimes running a red light will not hurt anyone. It would also require that we do away with all laws against theft because a starving man may need to steal a loaf of bread to feed his family. In fact, it would require that we do away with marriage itself because spouses in some marriages abuse one another and their children. But in doing that

73 See http://www.acpeds.org/?CONTEXT=art&cat=22&art=50&BISKIT=2920801063.

we'd be throwing the baby out with the bathwater. Natural marriage, as a whole, is great for society. We cannot let its exceptions prevent us from experiencing the overall benefits it produces. Natural marriage must remain our legal norm despite any exceptions to the rule.

Some marriages do not produce children.

Answer: Yes, but again they are the exception rather than the rule. The state recognizes marriage because marriage in general procreates and provides the most stable and nurturing environment for children. By the facts of nature, no homosexual act can do this—no exceptions.

Second, sterile heterosexual marriages still affirm the connection to childbearing because sterility is not generally known on the wedding day. And in those instances where sterility is known, as with older couples, the man-woman union still models what is generally a procreative relationship. There is a difference between having *old* plumbing and having the *wrong* plumbing.

Finally, it would not be possible or desirable for the state to attempt to determine which men and women are capable of procreation and which are not. However, since no homosexual relationship produces children, no homosexual relationship can fulfill this basic function of marriage.

Opposition to same-sex marriage is hate speech.

Answer: This assertion is utter nonsense, but unfortunately it carries the force of law in some countries that have adopted same-sex marriage. In fact, speech codes and "hate-crime" legislation seem to follow the approval of same-sex marriage. In Canada and Sweden, for example, speech is already restricted against homosexuality to the point that even pastors have been fined or jailed for quoting Bible verses![74] In the United States, Democrats continually put forth "hate-crime" legislation which may lead to the same result.[75]

Why do advocates of "hate-crime" legislation ignore the fact that *all* crimes are "hate" crimes (there are certainly no "love" crimes)? And why do they ignore the fact that *all* people—including homosexuals—are already protected equally under existing criminal law?

Perhaps it's because they are not really concerned with equal protection, fairness, or truth—they seek special protection because it will validate homosexual behavior. In other words, hate-crime legislation is about imposing political correctness, not punishing crime fairly. Why else would they advocate giving a stiffer punishment to a thug who beats up a homosexual than someone who beats up your grandmother? Since both crimes are terrible and both victims are equally human, the perpetrators should be punished equally. In fact, hate-crime legislation actually results in unequal protection. Homosexuals get more protection than you or anyone else. While you have civil rights, homosexuals get

---

74 Harry Jackson Jr., "The Massacre of the Pulpit," April 23, 2007, posted on-line at http://www.townhall.com/Columnists/HarryRJacksonJr/2007/04/23/the_massacre_of_the_pulpit.

75 Incidentally, in the Spring 2007 debate over HR 1592 (the House version of the Hate Crimes bill), one Republican wanted to add unborn children as a protected class to the bill; others wanted to add military personnel, senior citizens, and the homeless, but Democrats rejected those amendments. Why give extra protection to homosexuals and cross-dressers but not to our military, senior citizens, and homeless? Because this isn't about equal protection— it's about special protection that validates homosexual behavior. In fact, Congressman Mike Pence (R) of Indiana offered a Freedom of Religion amendment to ensure that the law would not limit the religious freedom of any person or group under the Constitution. But Democrats refused to adopt that as well.

super rights—rights that will trump any free speech or religion rights you have. "All opponents of same-sex marriage; you're under arrest!"[76]

Now, why isn't opposition to same-sex marriage hate speech? Because political disagreement is not hate speech. If it were, then homosexual activists would be guilty of hate speech toward heterosexuals for trying to change the definition of marriage. Moreover, disagreement with the radical gay political agenda does not make someone an enemy of homosexuals. I am opposed to the legal endorsement of a particular behavior. I am not opposed to the people who engage in that behavior. Just because we disagree about political ends does not mean we hate those who disagree with us.

Ironically, those of us who are reasonably pointing out the documented dangers of homosexual activity should be considered friends of homosexuals, not foes. After all, we are the ones trying to spare homosexuals from disease and death by telling the truth about the issue. Perhaps it is the activists who are suppressing that truth who are their real enemies.

We need to be tolerant.

Answer: Tolerance is not really the issue with our debate about homosexuality. Homosexual behavior is already legal in the United States. Again, the issue in this debate is whether we should we go beyond tolerance to endorsement.

---

76 For a good discussion of the problem with hate-crime legislation, see Greg Koukl, "Why Hate Shouldn't Be a Crime," Townhall.com, July 21, 2007, online at http://townhall.com/columnists/column.aspx?UrlTitle=why_hate_shouldnt_be_a_crime&ns=GregoryKoukl&dt=07/21/2007&page=full&comments=true.

It's one thing to permit homosexuality; it's quite another to promote it by endorsing same-sex marriage.

It is interesting to note, however, that when homosexual activists ask for tolerance, they are implicitly admitting that there's something wrong with their behavior. After all, you don't need to ask people to "tolerate" good behavior. Mother Teresa never had to ask for tolerance.

Tolerance is a virtue if you're talking about listening to other points of view, but it's a vice if you're talking about letting destructive behavior overrun your society. All civilized societies are intolerant of harmful behaviors such as murder, rape, and theft for example.

The truth is we are called to go beyond tolerance to love. Tolerance is too weak. Tolerance says, "Hold your nose and put up with them." Love says, "Reach out and help them." Love does not allow us to be indifferent to acts that destroy other people, and it certainly doesn't allow us to endorse such acts.

On a personal level, love demands that we reach out to the people involved in homosexuality. That includes accepting them as people but firmly standing against their destructive behavior. Tolerance of harmful behavior is unloving.

On a political level, love requires that we steadfastly oppose any legislation that would harm our society, including our children, our health, and our prosperity. As we have seen, government-backed same-sex marriage or civil unions would do just that by trivializing civilization's most basic institution—marriage itself. When tolerance morphs into endorsement in the form of same-sex marriage, the most loving thing to do is to oppose it.

Unfortunately, the tide of political correctness has risen so much that it is now conservatives who need to be requesting tolerance (and most of us are not doing anything wrong!). Homosexual activists have a double standard. They want us to endorse their ideas, but they will not tolerate even hearing ours. In fact, they don't even tolerate democracy or free speech when the results are not in their favor. That's why they're trying to impose their radical ideas on the people by circumventing the democratic process and going directly to the courts (they even went to court to block the people from voting on same-sex marriage in California). That's why they're also trying to silence any opposing view by seeking legislation that could make it a crime to speak out against homosexuality. They have succeeded in Canada and Sweden, and now they're pushing that same "non-discrimination" and "hate-crime" legislation here in America.

So according to homosexual activists, only people who oppose them have to be tolerant—they somehow have a moral right to impose their views on everyone else without anyone's consent. And if you disagree, you might be cited for a "hate-crime." For homosexual activists, tolerance is a one-way street.

You ought not judge!

Answer: Recently, I received an email from a lady who didn't like the case I made against same-sex marriage on our TV program (which airs on DirecTV channel 378). She wrote me the following e-mail with "VERY JUDGMENTAL" in the subject line:

Only God can judge me and I am a Christian lesbian and have been for almost 20 years. Stop judging and move on!!! I am so tired of all you uptight, do right, sinners judging people.

I responded this way:

Thanks for your comments. But are you judging me for judging? Indeed, it is impossible not to make judgments. The only question is, "Is your judgment correct?"

I would love to "move on" from this issue, but who is making this a front-burner issue? Not me, but homosexual activists who are making an aggressive attempt to get governments to endorse homosexuality by changing the definition of marriage.

We'll deal with objections next week. I hope you will watch with an open mind.

I could have added that it was not me but God who has already judged homosexual behavior as immoral. After all, God is the standard of morality, not me. But her response made it seem like she didn't know that. She wrote back that she would never watch again because I was "intolerant and wrong."

In effect, she did what many people do when they are faced with arguments they don't like—they ignore the arguments and misuse Jesus' apparent command not to "judge" in order to shut you up. So if you oppose their behavior or their attempt to get the nation to endorse their immorality (i.e. same-sex marriage), you're sure to hear, "Thou shalt not judge!"

As with most slogans shouted by such people, the truth is exactly opposite to what they claim. Those demanding tolerance take the judgment statements of Jesus out of context because they want to avoid any moral condemnation for their own actions, and they don't want you to notice that they are making judgments too. Let's take a look at what Jesus actually said:

> **"Do not judge lest you be judged.**
> **"For in the way you judge, you will be judged; and by your standard of measure, it will be measured to you.**
> **"And why do you look at the speck that is in your brother's eye, but do not notice the log that is in your own eye?**
> **"Or how can you say to your brother, 'Let me take the speck out of your eye,' and behold, the log is in your own eye?**
> **"You hypocrite, first take the log out of your own eye, and then you will see clearly to take the speck out of your brother's eye" (Matthew 7:1-5).**

Notice Jesus isn't telling us *not* to judge—Jesus is telling us *how* to judge. He commands us to take the speck out of our brother's eye—that involves making a judgment, but He also commands us to stop committing the bigger sins ourselves so we can better help our brother. In other words, when you judge, do so rightly, not hypocritically.

Jesus actually commands us to make judgments elsewhere in the Bible. In John 7:24, He says, "stop judging by mere appearances and make a right judgment." Jesus would never tell us to stop judging—that would be suicide. Just think about how impossible life would be if we did not make judgments. You make hundreds, if not thousands, of judgments every day between good and evil, right and wrong, dangerous choices from safe ones. You would be dead already if you did not make judgments. (Of course, there's a difference between making a judgment and being judgmental. We must make judgments, but we must make them with the right attitude.)

With regard to politics, every law is a judgment about what's best for society. Homosexual activists are making a judgment that same-sex marriage would be the best law for society. It's a wrong judgment, as I am arguing here, but it's a judgment nonetheless.

So in addition to being self-defeating, the belief that we "ought not judge" is completely impractical and even dangerous. Making judgments is unavoidable both personally and politically. If you want to meet a sudden and premature demise, just stop making judgments.

Unfortunately, homosexual activists are propelling our society toward a premature demise by making the disastrous judgment that we ought not to make judgments about their behavior. They, of course, can judge *our* behavior as immoral when we oppose same-sex marriage, but we are not to judge *their* behavior. This is exactly the kind of hypocrisy that Jesus warned against. The passage they quote actually convicts them.

For folks so concerned about the "separation of church and state," it is amazing how fast they will quote the Bible when they think it helps their case. But if they believe the Bible when they think it condemns judging (which it doesn't), then why don't they believe the Bible when it certainly condemns homosexuality? If they want to use the Bible as their standard, then they will be judged by that same standard.

Opposition to same-sex marriage is a violation of the separation of church and state.

Answer: I do not want the state running the church or the church running the state, but this objection completely misses the mark.

First, even if one were to accept the erroneous, court-invented claim that the Constitution requires a strict separation of church and state, opposition to same-sex marriage would not be unconstitutional. Churches and the Bible also teach that murder, rape, and child abuse are wrong, but no one says laws prohibiting such acts are a violation of the "separation of church and state." In fact, if the government could not pass laws consistent with church or biblical teachings, then all criminal laws would have to be overturned because they are all in some way consistent with at least one of the Ten Commandments.

Second, there are churches on both sides of this issue. In other words, *some churches actually support same-sex marriage.* So if there is a strict separation of church and state, then I suppose we cannot put the pro-same-sex marriage position into law either, right? Homosexual activists don't want to go there.

This "separation of church and state" objection involves a failure to distinguish between religion and morality. Religion involves our duty to God, while morality involves our duty to one another. Our lawmakers are not telling people how, when, or if to worship—that would be legislating religion. But lawmakers can't avoid telling people how they should treat one another—that's legislating morality.

As we point out in our book, *Legislating Morality*,[77] contrary to popular opinion, all laws legislate morality. Morality is about right and wrong, and every law legally declares one behavior right and its opposite wrong. So the question is not whether we can legislate morality; the question is, "Whose morality should we legislate?"

We should not legislate my morality or your morality, but *the* morality—the one we inherited, and not the one we invented; the one our founders declared is "self-evident" because it has been endowed on us by our Creator.

If you have a problem with *the* morality, don't blame me. I didn't make it up. I didn't make up the fact that men are not made for other men, or that sex outside of natural marriage leads to destruction. Those truths are part of the "Laws of Nature," as the Declaration of Independence puts it, and we only hurt ourselves and others by suppressing those truths so we can do what we want.

---

77 Frank Turek and Norman Geisler, *Legislating Morality*, (Eugene, Oregon: Wipf and Stock, 2003).

For thousands of years, we have legislated the self-evident truth that men are meant for women. Now suddenly homosexuals—long critical of conservatives for trying to "legislate morality"—are trying to legislate their own morality in the form of same-sex marriage. They want to ignore self-evident truths and impose their own invented morality on the entire country.

The only question is this: Should we continue to legislate the inherited morality that nurtures the next generation (natural marriage), or the invented one that entices it to destruction (same-sex marriage)? I think the answer is self-evident.

Don't put discrimination in the Constitution.

Answer: This is the slogan homosexual activists use to counter the proposed constitutional amendment to ban same-sex marriage. But this slogan is faulty as well. Discrimination is already in the Constitution. In fact, *all laws discriminate; but it is discrimination against behavior, not persons*, and it is discrimination with cause, not without.

For example, the First Amendment's "freedom of religion" protections discriminate against the behavior of some Muslims who want to impose Islam on the entire nation, but it does not discriminate against those Muslims as persons. The Thirteenth Amendment discriminates against the behavior of some businessmen who might like to improve their profits through slavery, but it does not discriminate against those businessmen as persons. Likewise, our marriage laws discriminate against the desired behaviors of homosexuals, polygamists, bigamists, adulterers, and the incestuous among us, but they do not discriminate against them as persons.

PART
IV

What We Must Do

Why Gay Reactions are Anything but Gay

A few years ago, I was in Chicago conducting a leadership seminar for a major insurance company. One of my fellow instructors—a woman I'll call Mary—announced to the attendees that she was a lesbian living with her partner. That led me into a friendly but rather lively exchange with her later that evening.

After a group of us had dinner, Mary and I were engaging in small talk in the lounge of the restaurant. Now, I really like Mary—she is outgoing, witty, and certainly good at her insurance profession. So when the other folks were a few feet out of earshot, I decided to ask her a little bit more about herself.

"Mary," I said, "Do you mind if I ask you a personal question?"

Since Mary is very direct, she was all for it.

"No, go ahead!" she said.

Being as discrete and unassuming as I could, I asked with a smile (you always have to smile in situations like this), "You mentioned that you're living with your partner. Do you find the gay lifestyle difficult? Has your family accepted it? Are they happy with it?"

Mary straightened up and adopted a more assertive tone.

"Of course they've accepted it! I come from a very enlightened family. They are very happy for me and just want me to be happy."

"What do you think about it?" she said, turning the tables on me, with a slight hint of a smile.

Since I'm very direct as well, I answered, "Forgive me, Mary, but I think it's wrong."

"You think it's wrong!" she fired back, eyebrows raised. Her tone was more confident than hostile. Like the lady who e-mailed me about our TV show, Mary then said, "Who are you to judge me, Frank?"

"Who are you to judge me for judging?" I countered.

As if I hadn't said a word, she repeated, "Who are you to judge me, Frank?"

"Mary," I said, leaning in for emphasis, "If we are not to judge, then why are you judging me for judging?"

Again, as if I was talking to a wall, she completely ignored my response. "I just think it's bigoted and intolerant of you not to accept my lifestyle," she announced.

"Are you bigoted and intolerant for not accepting my lifestyle?" I asked.

"But I do accept your lifestyle," she fired back.

"No, you don't," I told her. "Part of my lifestyle is to speak out against harmful behavior like homosexuality. You're intolerant of that, so you're judging me just as much as I'm judging you."

This verbal jousting went on for better than ten minutes. We had a civilized and friendly conversation, but Mary did what I find many people do when confronted with truth they don't like—they ignore it or suppress it. In Mary's case, she ignored it. She simply would not acknowledge that several of her claims were unreasonable because they were either self-defeating or hypocritical. For example, she told me to not judge but judged me in the process. She accused me of intolerance while being intolerant herself. Later in the conversation, she told me there are no moral absolutes, but then she went on to assert that tolerance and same-sex marriage are two moral absolutes that everyone must support.

Although she wouldn't acknowledge her inconsistency, Mary was at least pleasant to talk to. Many others, I've found, try to suppress the truth by getting hostile. They attack me rather than my arguments. Name-calling and profanity replace good reason. Nowadays, if you refuse to pretend that same-sex relationships are just as good as those of the opposite sex, you will be attacked personally. Ironically, the most intolerant folks are often those who say they are fighting for tolerance.

Why is this so? Because some people would rather follow their desires than follow the truth. They don't want to be changed by the truth. They want to do the impossible—they want to change the truth to validate their behavior. That's why they try to suppress the truth or the truth-teller.

Why else would someone attack me personally for citing the indisputable evidence that heterosexuality is more healthy and beneficial to society than homosexuality? I didn't make up those facts.

Why else would someone get emotional when I point out the obvious fact that men and women were designed for one another, but men-men or women-women were not? I didn't design the human body. I didn't invent what our founders called "The Laws of Nature."

Why else would someone get mad at me for highlighting the moral truth that if hurting other people is wrong, it's wrong even when it happens through homosexual sex? That's not my morality—I didn't make it up. I'm just citing the morality that is built into the very nature of the universe. In fact, aspects of that same moral code convict me as well. It teaches me to not hurt others, and there are many times I find that inconvenient. But since failing to live according to the morality brings grave consequences, it hurts us more in the long run to deny it, suppress it, or to attack those who remind us of it.

What is the point of me telling you all this? It's not to complain. If people want to call me and other same-sex marriage opponents names, that's fine. I'm telling you this to point out that this debate over same-sex marriage is not just an intellectual one. Since we are intellectual, emotional, and volitional beings, sometimes we allow our emotion and will to overrule the mind. In this debate you'll find too many people letting their emotions and will get in the way of sound thinking. They do not want to be confronted with the facts because those facts convict them. Again, as Augustine said, people love the truth when it enlightens them, but they hate it when it convicts them.

So if you oppose same-sex marriage, you will probably be tagged as an enemy of homosexuals by homosexual activists. They will not meet you with rational arguments for their position, but with hysterical cries that you are the next Hitler.[78] If history is any guide, they will put a swastika on me and anyone else who agrees with this book. Their propaganda machine will spew the most intolerant invectives you'll ever see. That's why so many conservatives shy away from this subject. No one wants to stomach the abuse.

This raises the question: Why do homosexual activists tend to be so mean-spirited? Is it just because they have no valid arguments? I think there's more to it than that.

---

78 Dr. Michael Brown, who has conducted very respectful dialogue with members of the homosexual community, experienced this name-calling firsthand. See his editorial to the *Charlotte Observer* reprinted here: http://www.coalitionofconscience.org/americasScapegoats.aspx. Of course, there are a few on the far right who also resort to name-calling. That's why I urge those on both sides of this debate to use arguments not slander. It's not only the right thing to do, but when we use arguments rather than slander natural marriage will win.

Think about how you react when you are exposed doing wrong. If you don't want to stop the behavior, the last thing you want is someone calling you on it. Those coming between you and your pet sin may feel the heat of your wrath, even though you know they are right.

This happened to me behind the wheel recently. I was running a little late and the person in front of me actually had the gall to drive the speed limit. Can you imagine? There I was trying to make up some time, and the person in front of me was actually obeying the law! Rage welled up inside of me. "You know you get the speed limit plus ten—let's go!"

I had to resist the nearly overwhelming urge to cross the double-yellow line and blow by him while screaming my best Jersey put down (yes, I'm originally from New Jersey). I resisted, but it was tough. The most alarming truth about the incident was that the feelings of rage came even though I knew he was right.

Now, imagine you have homosexual desires. Whether they are the result of nature or nurture is irrelevant. You have them, and you are tired of fighting them. Once you've made the choice to act on them, you'll probably seek others who've made the same choice because you want companionship and validation. How do you think you're going to feel about those who oppose your behavior? You might feel hatred toward them—or at least contempt—even though you know they're right. (In fact, if I felt rage driving, I would expect the feeling to be even more intense when related to sex—one of the most emotionally powerful and addictive acts in which we engage.)

Why does such rage seize us? It has to do with how the human conscience works. Our consciences don't just tell us what *is* right—they also urge us to *live* right. That means if we choose to live in a way that is against our consciences, we probably won't go peacefully on our merry way. The part of our conscience that urges us to live right will continue to convict us for suppressing the truth and living immorally. So we will aggressively seek rationalizations to prove to everyone, including ourselves, that we actually *are* living right.[79] Our conflicted consciences may boil over into rage against anyone who suggests our behavior is wrong. We simply can't tolerate anyone who calls attention to the truth we are suppressing. Their opposing views must be silenced.

By the way, this suppress-support-and-silence process is not unique to homosexuals. Most people who decide that they want to continue to defy their conscience will in some way suppress the truth, support their behavior with slick rationalizations, and then attempt to silence those who point out their errors. You've probably seen this if you've ever confronted an adulterer or a thief. They'll usually get defensive and come up with all sorts of excuses.

What makes homosexuals different, along with abortion rights advocates, is that they have been able to turn their pet sin into a political movement. It's difficult to convince people that adultery and theft should be legally endorsed behaviors, but moralizing slogans about "equality" and "choice" enable homosexuals and abortionists to

79 J. Budziszewski calls this "The Revenge of Conscience" in his book by the same name. The Apostle Paul describes the negative effects of sin on the mind in his letter to the Romans 1:18-32.

confuse enough people into thinking that they somehow have a right to homosexuality and abortion.

One prominent ex-homosexual admits to suppressing conscience and silencing all opposing views. Michael Glatze, the former editor of *Young Gay America* (the first gay magazine targeted at youth), gave up homosexuality after reflecting on his life and converting to Mormonism at age thirty. He writes, "God is regarded as an enemy by many in the grip of homosexuality or other lustful behavior, because He reminds them of who and what they truly are meant to be. People caught in the act would rather stay 'blissfully ignorant' by silencing truth and those who speak it, through antagonism, condemnation, and calling them words like 'racist,' 'insensitive,' 'evil,' and 'discriminatory.'"[80]

But it's more than just silencing conscience and opponents. It's also the outright denial of anything and everything that might diminish their justification of homosexuality. For example, I'm sure you've heard homosexual activists say that they would never choose to be homosexual if they had a choice. It's too painful and difficult a lifestyle to be chosen. So when thousands of former homosexuals say they've found a way out, you would expect homosexual activists to be happy for them and perhaps follow the same path, right? But that's not what they do at all. Instead, they vehemently deny that anyone can leave homosexuality.

For them, people like Michael Glatze and thousands of other ex-homosexuals[81] cannot exist because they disprove

---

80 Michael Glatze, "How a 'Gay Rights' Leader Became Straight," World Net Daily, July 3, 2007, available on-line at http://www.worldnetdaily.com/news/article.asp?ARTICLE_ID=56487.

81 For information on ex-homosexuals, go to http://www.exodus-international.org.

the movement's self-justifying assertion that desires or behavior can never change or be controlled. For them, Dr. Robert Spitzer, once their darling for getting homosexuality declassified as a mental disorder, must be berated for publishing scientific studies showing that some homosexuals have changed their orientation. Spitzer has been barraged with hate mail from enraged homosexuals simply for reporting the undeniable facts—facts which hurt their political cause.[82]

Why do homosexual activists say that they expect people with other desires—be they sexual or otherwise—to control themselves but put no restriction on their own behavior? Why do they expect those with gay-bashing desires to resist their desires? The double standard is blatant. While we all must restrain ourselves for the sake of civilization, homosexuals are entitled to toss off all restraint and demand from society not just tolerance, but endorsement of their harmful behavior.

Why do they demand endorsement? Because being tolerated does not quell the conscience. Only through society's full acceptance and approval will homosexuals be validated and their consciences quelled. Since they refuse to achieve approval by adhering to society's standards, they have no other choice but to change society's standards. That's why they are trying to beat society's marriage standards down to the level of their own behavior. All natural barriers must be annihilated. Only then will homosexuality have a chance of seeming natural and acceptable to a majority of people.

Their radical social revolution requires a radical political revolution. Homosexual activists aggressively recruit others

82 See Warren Throckmorton, PhD., "My interview with Dr. Robert Spitzer," posted online at http://www.drthrockmorton.com/interviewdrspitzer.pdf.

who have made the same or similar choices and deny that anyone can go back (despite thousands of disconfirming examples). That's why they are in bed politically with pedophiles, cross-dressers, and the transgendered of the world. Anyone willing to fight for their own brand of sexual perversion is another soldier in their revolutionary army to destroy and remake sexual norms in their image.

Now that they have their army, they are conducting an all-out "in your face" campaign to redefine right and wrong in the minds of mainstream society. The more they suppress the truth and indulge in the behavior, the shriller they become defending it. Forget the effects it will have on marriage and children. Forget the effects it will have on health. Forget the effects it will have on prosperity. Everything must change to accommodate them!

J. Budziszewski exposes their scorched-earth crusade this way: "The shape of human life must be transformed. All of the assumptions of normal sexuality must be dissolved: marriage, family, innocence, purity, childhood—all must be called into question, even if it means pulling down the world around their ears."[83]

Remember, such "subversive" action is exactly what homosexual activists like Michelangelo Signorile urge for the movement. He and 96 percent of homosexuals do not want to get "married." What they want to do is to "transform the notion of 'family'" and "alter the archaic institution" of natural marriage. They are going to do that by imposing same-sex marriage through the courts so the people don't have a say.

83 J. Budziszewski, *What We Can't Not Know*, (Dallas: Spence, 2003), pg. 153.

Protecting Natural Marriage: Our National Immune System

Let me go back to my childhood friend for a minute. It was after high school that he went to New York City and immersed himself so deeply in the homosexual lifestyle that it cost him his life. We buried him at the age of thirty-six, dead from AIDS.

Actually, AIDS did not kill him. As you know, Acquired Immune Deficiency Syndrome technically doesn't kill anyone. AIDS destroyed his immune system, which made him susceptible to other diseases. Pneumonia and other ailments were the ultimate cause of death. In the end, he became a shell of his former self. On his deathbed, his mind was so tainted by dementia that he cursed his own mother.

As I mentioned, his loving and well-meaning parents made a tragic mistake. Love requires that we stand in opposition to sexual behavior that will likely hurt or kill our loved ones. Yet after some initial hesitancy, these well-meaning parents endorsed the homosexual lifestyle that ultimately led to their son's death. They thought they were being compassionate and loving, but they were really enabling a tragedy.

This tragic story is being played out right now on the national level. The players are different, but the results could be the same if we make the same mistake. Homosexual activists, buoyed by activist state Supreme Court rulings that they initiated, want our nation to endorse same-sex marriage. If they succeed and establish government-backed same-sex marriage or civil unions, our country will be doing exactly what those well-meaning parents did—they will be endorsing a practice that could destroy our immune system. On the national scale, our immune system is natural marriage itself. When our marriages are strong, our country is strong. When they are weak, we all suffer.

That's why we need to oppose same-sex marriage. If we allow our emotional affection for our gay friends and relatives to interfere with sound reasoning, we risk making the same mistake of false compassion that my friend's parents made—endorsing behavior that will hurt our loved ones and ourselves. But our mistake will not hurt just one person—it will hurt future generations repeatedly.

Homosexual activists work hard to suppress the fact that same-sex marriage would be a disaster for future generations. They cannot let truth get in the way of their desire to be "liberated" from the oppressive laws of marriage.

But they might as well talk about being "liberated" from the oppressive laws of physics. Like the laws of physics, the laws of marriage are not arbitrary laws that we can ignore without consequences. They are part of the immutable design of nature, and we hurt ourselves and others by pretending that they are merely human constructs. Those who attempt to "liberate" themselves from the design of nature usually wind up liberating themselves from good health and even life itself. As we have seen, homosexuals are no exception.

We need to face the facts of our design. When we do, we will realize that homosexual and heterosexual relationships can never be equal, and our laws should not be changed to pretend they are. After all, laws can't change the facts of nature. A new law can't magically transfer the natural procreative abilities of men and women, and the benefits of natural marriage, to homosexuals—nor can it erase the serious health problems that result from homosexual behavior. A new law approving same-sex marriage would only serve to deceive people into thinking that same-sex marriage and natural marriage are equally beneficial. Such legally-endorsed deception would be a dangerous teacher to new generations. Yet that deception is exactly what homosexual activists are counting on to validate their lifestyle.

Government-backed same-sex marriage will teach future generations these *false* ideas:

- Homosexual behavior is just as beneficial as heterosexual behavior;
- Same-sex marriage is just as beneficial as natural marriage;
- Moms and dads offer nothing uniquely beneficial to the care and development of children (homosexual couples *always* deny children either their mom or dad);
- Marriage is no longer about procreation, just coupling. Therefore, if you want to have children, there is really no reason to get married.

These are false and dangerous ideas. Those who promote them stand to hurt themselves and others. Only natural marriage can secure a healthy future for our children and our entire civilization. Therefore, it alone deserves privileged legal support.

Despite what our homosexual loved ones may want, we must not make the same mistake as my friend's parents.

Love requires that we stand firm and not succumb to false compassion. The most loving policy for them and the rest of our country is to legally protect marriage—our national immune system. Outside of impeaching activist judges (which is our best option), a constitutional amendment appears to be the most practical way to ensure that marriage remains solely the union of one man and one woman.

If You Are Still Not Convinced

Perhaps you believe that there are good arguments for same-sex marriage. I honestly have not seen any, but I could be missing something. David Blankenhorn lists what he thinks are some good pro-same-sex marriage arguments in his book. Blankenhorn, a liberal democrat who is generally pro-gay, believes that those arguments are not nearly as weighty as those against same-sex marriage.

In an interview with *USA Today*, Blankenhorn explains, "I'm not condemning homosexuality. I'm not condemning committed gay relationships. [But] the best institutional friend that children have is marriage, and if grown-ups make a mess of it, the children are going to suffer."[84] Indeed, he realizes that the welfare of children is more important than validating the sexual desires of some adults.

By opposing same-sex marriage, Blankenhorn is not selling out his gay friends. I have argued that he is actually helping them. Even if he's not helping them—even if gay behavior were just as healthy as straight behavior—we

84 Sharon Jayson, "Blankenhorn: A Family Guy with a Cause," *USA Today*, March 14, 2007. Posted online at http://www.americanvalues.org/html/FUMA.htm.

would still be right in opposing same-sex marriage in order to protect children and the country.

In some public policy debates there are no perfect solutions, only tradeoffs. The lower value must give way to the higher. Even if you think there are some good reasons to support same-sex marriage, and even if you think some of my arguments are flawed, it is still perfectly reasonable to support the constitutional amendment banning same-sex marriage to achieve the greater good for children and the country.

Some will say, "But marriage is an issue for the states. Why are you trying to get the federal government involved?" It is true that marriage law has long been an issue for the states. And many states have passed and should continue to pass bans on same-sex marriage. However, lawsuits from homosexual activists continually threaten your ability to decide the issue at the ballot box. Because of these lawsuits, a few unelected justices from the Massachusetts and California Supreme Courts have made same-sex marriage a federal issue by making up rights that aren't in either state constitution. Either of those two activist rulings have the potential to become the law of every other state through the "full faith and credit clause" of the United States Constitution.

Article IV, Section 1 of the U.S. Constitution states, "Full faith and credit shall be given in each state to the public acts, records, and judicial proceedings, of every other State." In other words, if one state recognizes same-sex marriage, a suit in federal court may force other states to recognize those marriages as well, even if the people in those other states have voted to ban same-sex marriage in their own state constitutions. In effect, the U.S. Constitution would overrule all the state constitutions. This is how just a few unelected state judges can impose their own views on the entire country and why an amendment to the U.S. Constitution is necessary.

Think of that—a few unelected justices in one state can, in effect, change the laws of the entire country. Talk about discrimination—that's discrimination against the other three hundred million people in this country who are entitled to govern themselves! When any court oversteps its bounds and usurps the will of the people by legislating from the bench, the only sure remedy is to ignore the court and impeach the justices. Since most politicians are too scared to do that, our next best bet is an amendment to the United States Constitution. Of course, judges could ignore that new part of the Constitution too, as they have ignored so many old parts. But at least the constitutional amendment process would involve the American people making it more difficult for any rogue court to get away with ignoring their will so blatantly.

It is revealing to note that homosexuals rely on the courts to get them the social approval they crave because they know that they cannot win such approval by a fair vote of the people. Until the Massachusetts and California Supreme Courts overstepped their authority, "we the people" have decided which sexual relationships are worthy of legal recognition and which are not. And "we the people" have done so not on arbitrary grounds, but in light of the natural design and compatibility of a man and a woman and all of the benefits that come from their union. In other words, we legally recognize and confer benefits on man-woman unions because only natural marriage benefits our society at large.

Americans, like every civilized people before us, have put marriage alone in a privileged class because marriage alone is supremely beneficial.

It has been said that before you move a fence, you should pause long enough to see why it was placed there in the first place. Activist courts don't pause. They do whatever they want and whatever is politically correct at the time. Our legislative process was designed to be slow and deliberative to reduce the likelihood of someone moving an important fence in the middle of the night. That's why we need to urge the legislature to take back control. When we pause long enough to set aside emotion and look at the facts, we can see that unless we impeach judges, a constitutional amendment is necessary to protect our national immune system.

Conclusion: Is it Right?

Homosexual activists like to paint conservatives like myself as haters who condemn gays. But from my religious perspective, I am just as condemned as anyone else. I believe that everyone does wrong, including me, and that I am called to hate everything harmful and wrong in someone's life while unconditionally loving that person as a person. In fact, the way to love a person is to hate what is destroying them.

But we are not talking about sin and salvation here; we are talking about public policy. As with all public policy debates, the debate over same-sex marriage is about the standard of behavior that we ought to endorse for the good of the nation. In other words, it's not about whether you like or dislike homosexuals, or whether you consider their behavior sinful or not; it's about what would—to employ the logic of our Constitution—"promote the general welfare" of the nation as a whole. As we have seen, the best way to do that is to promote natural marriage and prohibit any endorsement of same-sex relationships.

Unless we do something to stop the same-sex marriage train, we will soon be endorsing homosexuality and degrading natural marriage in the process. That's because homosexual activists are just that—active. They are not taking a "live-and-let-live" approach with society. They want to impose their radical views on the entire country, and their all-out assault will hurt our children, our health, and our prosperity.

Some may say, "Well, same-sex marriage is legal now in Massachusetts, and the sky hasn't fallen there." That is because the cultural damage doesn't arrive overnight. It sometimes takes years for legal changes to affect the culture. But make no mistake—that damage will come. In the United States, we are paying now for the liberalization of divorce laws that occurred about forty years ago. In some of the aforementioned countries overseas, they are paying now for their affirmation of same-sex marriage a decade or so ago.

How about you? Will you enable the destruction of society by succumbing to political correctness—by saying and doing nothing? Edmund Burke said, "The only thing necessary for evil to prevail is for good people to do nothing." Indeed, 3 percent with passion will rule the 97 percent who are apathetic and choose to do nothing. Will you do nothing or will you stand up and be counted? In case you are tempted to do nothing, I urge you to consider the words of Dr. Martin Luther King:

> *Cowardice asks the question, 'Is it safe?'*
> *Expediency asks the question, 'Is it political?'*
> *Vanity asks the question, 'Is it popular?'*
> *But conscience asks the question, 'Is it right?'*

And there comes a time when one must take a position that is neither safe, nor political, nor popular, but one must take it because one's conscience tells one that it is right."

As we have seen, the evidence shows it is right to support natural marriage and oppose same-sex marriage. Do you have the courage to do so? For the sake of your country and your children and grandchildren, you must.

For Those of You Who Are Now Offended

Some of you may now accuse me of being too strident or insensitive in my treatment of this subject. I have tried to respond to arguments, not attack individuals. I certainly hope that I've been sensitive to people who struggle with homosexual desires. If I have erred, forgive me.

However, it is better to be correct than politically correct. I would rather err on the side of being insensitive than risk being an enabler of destructive behavior. A friend of mine died, partially because no one stood for the truth. And thousands of others have died or have been harmed across America, partially because too few of us stood for the truth.

Given the stakes, it is time we speak the truth clearly about this issue rather than tiptoe around it. If we inadvertently offend some who are overly-sensitive, so be it. In fact, if you have taken offense to something I've said, ask yourself, "But is it true?" If it is and you're still offended, there's nothing I or anyone can do to change the truth.

By the way, if you are offended by the truth, you don't really have a problem with me or other same-sex marriage opponents. We did not design the human body and how it works. You have a problem with the Designer and the facts of nature.

Second, instead of claiming that you are offended, did you ever consider that you are offending an entire nation by advocating the destruction of the very foundation of civilization, and that you are trying to achieve this destruction not by a fair vote of the people, but by imposing it on them through lawsuits and rogue judges? If you want to change something, then convince people at the ballot box.

Finally, if you knowingly endorse destructive behavior, you need to be challenged and your position needs to be defeated. It is my hope that the direct approach I've taken here will help you acknowledge what you already know to be true: *Homosexual and heterosexual relationships are not the same, can never be the same, and will never yield the same benefits to individuals or society. We hurt everyone by pretending otherwise.*

PART V

After the Supreme Court: What Now?

Fallacies do not cease being fallacies when they become fashions.
— G.K. Chesterton

Since the first edition of this book in 2008, I've written several columns addressing the issues that have risen around same-sex marriage, including my own firing from two major companies for writing this book. I've updated some of those columns here.

I'll start by calling out Christians. If you're upset with where the country is morally, before you blame liberals you might want to blame the church.

Is the Country a Mess? Blame the Church

As our great country accelerates its slide into an economic and moral hell, be careful whom you blame. The present boldness of liberals and the timidity of conservatives are only the secondary causes. Much of the blame can be placed at the foot of the church.

When I say the church, I don't mean an institution like the Roman Catholic church, but the entire body of believers—those from all denominations who believe that the Bible is true, that people are sinners, that God sent the perfect God-man, Jesus Christ, to redeem us from our sins, and that we are charged with spreading that message and reforming society.

Believers are God's ambassadors here on earth, called to be salt and light *in* the world and *to* the world. When we follow our calling, individuals are transformed and societies with them. Our country is failing because too many believers have abandoned this calling.

They began abandoning it in earnest in the 1920s. An anti-intellectual movement called fundamentalism led believers to separate from society rather than reform it, and to bifurcate life into two separate spheres—the sacred and secular. Reason was given up for emotionalism, and only activities that directly saved souls were deemed sacred. Everything else was considered secular. Careers in clergy and missions were glorified at the expense of everything else. That led to many believers to leave public education, the media, law, and politics in the hands of the unbelievers. Is it any wonder why those areas of our culture now seem so godless? Take God's influence out and that's what you get.

Secularizing public education has been the key to our nation's moral demise. Once public education went secular, the rest of society eventually followed, especially when the products of that system became our leaders. As Abraham Lincoln once observed, "The philosophy of the schoolroom in one generation will be the philosophy of the government in the next."

The philosophy of the schoolroom is atheistic. The question of God's existence—the most important question regarding how we should live—is not studied or debated in our public schools. Atheism is assumed to be true and with it moral relativism. That's a major reason why immorality dominates our schools and why our kids know more about political correctness than truth. It's also why we have a new generation of voters more enamored with "hope and change" than defending our changeless rights from an overreaching government. G.K. Chesterton's observation about Russia has come true here, "Once abolish the God, and the government becomes the God."

How did this happen? In the early 1960s, the Supreme Court, consisting of newly trained secularists, banned devotional Bible reading in our schools (apparently for the one hundred and eighty years before that, people just didn't understand the Constitution!). That decision, and several others, has stifled virtually any mention of God or the Bible in our public schools. In effect, the most influential book in the history of the world is ignored in our educational system. What kind of a quality education is that? It's certainly not what the folks who settled this land had in mind for public education. In fact, the first public school in the new world began as a result of the "Old Deluder Satan Law." This 1647 Massachusetts law established the school to teach kids how to read the Bible so that old deluder Satan could not deceive them.

Likewise, most of our first universities were established to teach and propagate a complete Christian worldview. As Harvard's "rules and precepts" in 1646 read:

> *Let every Student be plainly instructed, and earnestly pressed to consider well, the main end of his life and studies is, to know God and Jesus Christ which is eternal life (John 17:3) and therefore to lay Christ in the bottom, as the only foundation of all sound knowledge and Learning.*

The founders of Harvard knew that all truth is God's truth. There is no bifurcation between the sacred and the secular. According to the Bible, every vocation, every discipline, and every person is sacred. Nothing is secular. In sharp contrast, those running our country now say that everything is secular. That's a long way from our founding.

"So what?" you say. "Who cares about morality and God?"

That's exactly the problem—who does care? When the church separates from society, it takes its moral influence with it. But respect for the moral principles upon which our nation was founded—life, liberty, and the pursuit of happiness—are essential to its survival. Our founders knew this.

Following the Constitutional convention, a woman asked Benjamin Franklin what kind of government he and his fellow Founding Fathers created for the nation. Franklin replied, "A republic, if you can keep it."

Franklin knew that freedom must always be defended. He understood that the unalienable rights for which our

Founding Fathers pledged "their lives, fortunes, and sacred honor" were not secure unless an informed electorate held their representatives accountable to uphold those moral rights.

Recognizing that only a religious and moral people would maintain a good government, George Washington declared in his farewell address, "Of all the dispositions and habits which lead to political prosperity, Religion and Morality are indispensable supports." His successor, John Adams, wrote, "Our Constitution was made only for a moral and religious people. It is wholly inadequate to the government of any other." In other words, even the best Constitution cannot prevent immoral people or politicians from destroying a nation. That's why the church cannot abandon its calling—but it has.

So if you're a believer who is upset that life is not being protected; that marriage is being subverted; that judges routinely usurp your will; that our immigration laws are being ignored; that radical laws are passed but never read; that mentioning God in school (unless He's Allah) results in lawsuits; that school curriculum promotes political correctness and sexual deviance as students fail at basic academics; that unimaginable debt is being piled on your children while Planned Parenthood receives your tax dollars; and that your religion and free speech rights are about to be eroded by "hate" crimes legislation that can punish you for quoting the Bible; then go look in the mirror and take your share of the blame because we have not obeyed our calling.

Then start over. Reengage at every level of society. Treat every job and every person as sacred. Be a beacon for Christ and truth wherever you are and in whatever you do. There is hope if you act. After all, we believe in redemption.

The Supreme Court Decision: Love Didn't Win—Children Lost

"Love Wins" is the hashtag of choice for those in support of the newest Supreme Court decision (*Obergefell v. Hodges*) that passed that legislative body by a 5-4 vote. If you're not content with that, you're just an evil bigot who needs to shut up and support this new legislation. Forget the fact that you have very rational reasons for keeping marriage between a man and a woman. Genderless marriage changes the cultural understanding of marriage from the well being of children to merely the romantic desires of adults.

Same-sex marriage institutionalizes missing parents. In other words, *same-sex marriage legally promotes the idea that missing a mom or a dad is a good thing!* For kids who all deserve a mom and a dad and need a culture to support that, love hasn't won.

But you are to pay no attention to the children behind the curtain! If you don't change your bigoted position (which isn't really bigoted) many in the "Love Wins" crowd will bully you into submission. Although they say they are for tolerance and against bullying, they will see to it that you are fired, fined, sued, run out of business, and forced to violate your conscience and God. If this is "love," I'd hate to see what hate looks like!

Each side on this issue believes the other side is wrong. Whether you are for or against redefining marriage, there is a moral judgment made. Morality is always legislated (or judicially imposed). So what is the right morality?

The Supreme Court has told us. Five justices imposed their own morality that elevates homosexuality as a virtue in our society. They say states can't merely permit homosexual behavior (a neutral position). States must now promote it by granting benefits and, in Justice Kennedy's words, "dignity" through the most "profound" union of marriage.

Those who don't agree with this new morality imposed by the court are, in effect, the new sinners motivated by "disrespect" and "animosity." "Animosity" comes from Kennedy's *Lawrence* decision—a precedent he cited to justify his own animosity toward opponents of genderless marriage. Yes, unfortunately the Court smears all opponents to its new morality with the same judgmental bigotry it says it detests.

This raises a profound question that is central to this decision and every decision we make in politics. What is our standard? By what standard do we judge something as right and its opposite as wrong? By what standard do five justices elevate homosexuality to a virtue and declare any opposition to that position as "animosity" and "disrespect" toward people who identify as homosexual?

The standard should have been the Constitution, but the Constitution was ignored in this case. Justice Roberts rightfully wrote in his dissent, "The Constitution had nothing to do with it." While the majority said they consulted the Constitution, Kennedy actually spent most of his opinion citing his own horrendously argued previous opinions that also ignored or distorted the real Constitution.

When you look at the real Constitution (the one the people actually passed, not the "evolving" one invented in the minds of politically motivated judges), it's easy to see why this court is wrong. When the 14th Amendment was passed in 1868, homosexual behavior was a felony in every state, and women and blacks didn't even have the right to vote. If the "equal protection" clause of the 14th Amendment didn't even ensure a woman's right to vote, it certainly doesn't ensure a woman's right to marry another woman!

By Kennedy's own admission just two years ago in the *Windsor* decision, marriage is a state, not a federal, issue (unless a law violates the 14th Amendment's prohibition of *racial* discrimination, something that was not in play in this case). Now suddenly two years later, Kennedy, along with his mini-legislature, decides that everyone, including himself, has been interpreting the 14th Amendment incorrectly for one hundred forty-seven years!

Want to give women and blacks the right to vote? Then amend the Constitution (which the people did). Want to make marriage a federal rather than a state issue, and change it into a genderless institution? Then the people need to amend the Constitution.

But the Court decided to ignore all that. Kennedy and his anti-democracy cohorts decided that *they* were the new standard. Not the Constitution. Not the people. Not God or His natural law that gives us the "self-evident" truth that homosexual and heterosexual relationships are profoundly different in many ways, most importantly by their capacity to create and nurture children.

The personal opinions of five unelected justices now comprise the new standard that 320 million people must obey. That's right friends, after telling us in 1992 that everyone had "the right to define one's own concept of existence, of meaning, of the universe, and of the mystery of human life," Justice Kennedy and his cohorts have abandoned that self-defeating psychobabble and imposed on the entire nation their own meaning of marriage. Even if you are for genderless marriage, the fact that five unelected people think that their personal opinions are the standard for the rest of us should scare you.

If five people can ignore the Constitution and redefine the institution that holds together the foundation of civilization—the biological two-parent family—then no law or liberty is safe. That includes free speech and the free exercise of religion. (They are coming after those right now.)

"Oh, but we have the Bill of Rights," you say. "They can't take those away."

They already have to a certain extent. The issues reserved for the people and the states—which include marriage and almost everything else—have been taken from us by the mini-legislature. With this group it doesn't matter what the Constitution actually says. It doesn't matter what laws you pass or what the words mean. It doesn't matter that we are supposed to be governed by the rule of law not the whims of men. The whims of five people are now supreme—unless governors decide to evoke the Tenth Amendment and nullify this decision for their states, which they should. Is there a governor who will save this country from an imperial court? Is there an Andrew Jackson in a governor's mansion anywhere?

The words of John Adams couldn't be more fitting: "Our Constitution was made only for a moral and religious people. It is wholly inadequate to the government of any other."

Love hasn't won—the immoral gods on the Supreme Court changed its definition, and children, democracy, and America lost.

The Short Case Against Same-Sex Marriage: The four P's and two Q's

If you only have a few minutes to discuss the issue of same-sex marriage with someone, I recommend that you concentrate on the four P's and two Q's.

The first P deals with the government's **PURPOSE** in being involved in marriage in the first place. The government has not been involved in marriage because two people have romantic feelings for or love one another. Why would the government care about romance? The primary purpose the government has for being involved in promoting marriage between a man and a woman is because only that relationship can perpetuate and stabilize society. No other relationship has the biological or parenting diversity to best create and nurture the next generation. Sorry, but those are the facts of nature.

The next three P's deal with the three options the government has in addressing any behavior. The government can **PROHIBIT** a behavior, it can **PERMIT** a behavior, or it can **PROMOTE** a behavior.

For many years our laws *prohibited* sexual relationships like polygamy, incest, and pedophilia. They *permitted* homosexual relationships and non-marital heterosexual relationships. Due to the immense benefits the committed union of a man and a woman brings society, our laws *promoted* marriage between a man and woman. Notice that even prior to the Supreme Court decision, any two people in our society were already *permitted* to commit themselves to one another until death do them part. Since they didn't need the government to do that, this debate has not been about tolerance. Same-sex relationships were already tolerated.

Here's why promoting natural marriage exclusively does not deny anyone equal rights.

First, everyone has the same equal right to marry a qualified person of the opposite sex. That law treats every man and woman equally, but not every *behavior* they may desire equally. Same-sex marriage and natural marriage are different behaviors with different outcomes, so the law rightfully treats them differently. One behavior perpetuates and stabilizes society and the other doesn't. Promoting one behavior does not deny rights to people who don't engage in that behavior.

An analogy may help clarify this point. Like marriage, the government *promotes* police work by paying people to become police officers because police do much good for society. If you can't qualify to become a police officer, or if you choose another vocation, are your rights violated when the government pays other people to be police officers? Of course not—all people, regardless of their vocation, experience the benefits of police. Likewise, all people, regardless of their marriage status, experience the benefits of natural marriage.

Second, the law addresses behaviors, not persons. In other words, good laws treat all persons equally, but not necessarily what persons *do* equally. People may be born with certain sexual inclinations or acquire them later in life, but that's irrelevant to what the law should be. Laws deal with actions, not attractions—with what people *do*, not what they feel like doing. That's why the parallels to the civil rights struggles regarding race are fallacious. Skin color is not a behavior, but same-sex relations and same-sex marriage *are* behaviors. You will find many former homosexuals but you will never find a former African-American, Hispanic, or Caucasian.

Third, everyone puts limits on marriage—if marriage had no definition it wouldn't be anything. Even most same-sex marriage proponents want to define marriage in such a way so groups cannot marry and relatives cannot marry. *Are those homosexual activists bigots when they advocate that marriage not include groups, relatives, or other parties?* Of course not! They are not violating anyone's rights. Likewise, conservatives who advocate that marriage not include same-sex relationships are not violating anyone's rights. Defining marriage in accordance with the facts of nature is not bigotry—it's biology.

Some will ignore those biological realities and object, "But men and women are the same so there's no difference between homosexual and heterosexual relationships!"

If that were true, no one would be arguing for same-sex marriage. *The fact that people demand same-sex marriage is precisely because they know men and women are drastically different.* If men and women were the same, no one would have spent the time and energy trying to get same-sex marriage approved. They would have simply married someone of the opposite sex—which according to them is the same as someone of the same-sex—and be done with it.

Why not promote both natural marriage *and* same-sex marriage? Several reasons, but I can only briefly mention three.

First, same-sex marriage makes the institution of marriage genderless. There are *not* now two forms of marriage—natural and same-sex—but marriage legally and culturally is now a genderless institution about merely coupling. In the U.S., it's Partner A and Partner B. In other words, same-sex marriage divorces children from marriage. The law is a great teacher, and same-sex marriage teaches that marriage is about adult desires, not the needs of children. Marriage should be more about what children need than what adults want. If marriage isn't about the needs of children, then what institution *is* about children and the next generation? So homosexuality really isn't the issue here—making marriage genderless and childless is.

Second, since natural marriage and same-sex marriage are different behaviors with different outcomes they should not be equated legally. To see this, consider the two Q's:

Q1: ***How would society benefit if everyone lived faithfully in natural marriage?*** It would benefit everyone in society because it would result in a massive reduction in poverty, crime, child abuse, welfare, and government spending.

Q2: *How would society benefit if everyone lived faithfully in same-sex marriage?* It would be the end of society itself.

Now, I am *not* suggesting that a law would fully achieve either, but I am pointing out that natural and same-sex marriage should not be legally or culturally equated. The truth is homosexual and heterosexual relationships are not the same, can never be the same, and will never yield the same benefits to individuals or society. We hurt everyone, especially children, by pretending otherwise.

Finally, as we are now seeing, people lose their freedoms of speech, association, religion, and even parenting rights due to the imposition of same-sex marriage. The LGBT community not only wants to force curriculum upon children, they want florists, caterers, photographers, and even pastors to participate in their same-sex ceremonies!

Question: why would you want anyone who didn't agree with your wedding to be at your wedding? If you want to force people to participate in your wedding, then your wedding is less about celebrating a commitment and more about punishing those who can't in good conscience celebrate with you. Why can't you have your right to celebrate, while others maintain their right to not?

To sum up, the government already *permits* homosexual relationships, but *promoting* them by equating them with married heterosexual relationships ignores the facts of nature, the needs of children, and the health of society. While people with different sexual attractions are equal, not all *behaviors* are equally beneficial. True equality treats equal behaviors equally. It doesn't demand that different behaviors be treated the same.

The basic difference between conservatives and liberals is this: *Conservatives want to change their behavior to fit reality, while liberals want to change reality to fit their behavior.* The liberal approach, however well-intended, is a fool's errand guaranteed to end in disaster, both on an individual and national scale.

If these observations make you mad, don't blame me. I wish I could affirm same-sex marriage, but I didn't make up the facts of nature. Conservatives, like myself, are simply observing that society will be better off if we conserve policies consistent with what we know about the facts of nature and the importance of natural marriage to civilization.

If you are mad at me it means that in an important sense, you agree with me. If you don't like the behaviors and ideas I am advocating here, you are admitting that all behaviors and ideas are *not* equal—that some are closer to the real objective truth than others. The objective truth is that good political laws don't ignore objective natural laws. We can't change the facts of nature by passing laws. Good laws attempt to conform our desired behavior to reality—they do not attempt to conform reality to our desired behavior.

Sex at Work?

Are you supposed to have sex at work? I guess it depends on your profession, but for most of us the answer is "no." Why then is corporate America obsessed with training about sex?

In 2011, I was fired as a consultant from Cisco and Bank of America for my conservative beliefs about sex and marriage even though my beliefs were never expressed on the job. Let me tell you what happened at Cisco.

When a homosexual manager found out on the Internet that I had authored the book you're reading right now (the first edition was published in 2008), he couldn't tolerate me and requested I be fired. An HR executive canned me within hours without ever speaking to me or reading the book. This happened despite the fact that the leadership and team building programs I led always received high marks—even from the homosexual manager!

How could an experienced HR professional commit such a blatant act of discrimination *unless* the Cisco culture was decidedly tilted left? Why didn't Cisco's relentless emphasis on training on "inclusion and diversity" serve to prevent this? Maybe it's because "inclusion and diversity" means something different to corporate elites than to normal Americans. That's why their training didn't prevent the problem but actually created an environment of intolerance that led to the problem.

Cisco's chief "Inclusion and Diversity" officer, Ms. Marilyn Nagel, had trouble on the phone defining what "inclusion and diversity" actually means at Cisco, so she sent me several links from the Cisco website. As in our conversation, I found no specific definition on the website but plenty of platitudes, such as Cisco is committed to "valuing and encouraging different perspectives, styles, thoughts, and ideas."

If that's the case, then why not value my "perspectives, styles, thoughts, and ideas?"

Because only certain perspectives, styles, thoughts and ideas are approved, you see. "Inclusion and diversity" to corporate elites actually means *exclusion* for those that don't agree with the approved views. Whoops, there goes "diversity."

Shouldn't the real intent of Cisco's value of "inclusion and diversity" be to ensure that people in that diverse workforce work together cordially and professionally even when they inevitably disagree on certain political, moral, or religious questions? It would seem so. In a large multicultural workforce, people need to work together despite political or religious differences. That's a noble and necessary goal. It's totalitarian, however, to subject people to "diversity" training that goes beyond teaching respect for people *to advocacy of what they do in bed.*

All employees should treat one another with kindness and respect *because they are fellow human beings*, not because of their sexual behavior. If people are to be respected simply on the basis of their behavior, then none of us qualify for respect because we have all behaved badly on occasion.

So instead of trying to force all employees to accept any sexual behavior—especially something as controversial as homosexuality—the inclusion and diversity police should be urging us to treat all people with respect simply because we are human beings. That's all you need to be productive at work anyway.

As soon as you start telling people from different religious and cultural backgrounds what they must think about homosexuality, you will offend and create conflict and resentment. As a Christian, I am commanded to respect all people. That's what I was doing at Cisco. But don't tell me that I have to respect and celebrate what people do in bed. Don't tell me that I must violate my conscience or God in order to make widgets. That's not only immoral and un-American, it's manipulative and stupid. How does accepting homosexual *behavior* have anything to do with job productivity? Are we supposed to have sex at work?

There simply is no business reason to judge my beliefs about sexual behavior or anyone else's. Even if some corporate nanny could dream up a reason, it would not justify the assault on an employee's conscience or religion.

Notice that Cisco did not have a problem with my behavior. My job performance was deemed excellent, and I was "inclusive and diverse" by working in a respectful manner with people of all moral, religious, and political views.

Cisco had a problem with my thoughts. Although I certainly accepted homosexuals, I committed the thought crime of disagreeing with homosexual *behavior* and homosexual political goals. So despite all their talk about "inclusion and diversity," Cisco deemed my thoughts about something irrelevant to the workplace as grounds for immediate exclusion. Do you think they would have excluded me if I had pro-same-sex marriage thoughts? Of course not—that's an approved view that Cisco actually sponsored in 2011, even though they denied it to me.

But then people who don't accept homosexual behavior don't have to work at Cisco!

True, they don't. But if Cisco or any other company wants to make it a requirement that every employee and vendor personally accept the behavior of homosexuality or homosexual political goals, such as same-sex marriage, then tell us directly. Broadcast it to the world. Cisco can't and won't because such a requirement would be a clear violation of the religious protections codified in the Civil Rights Act, and it would result in a mass exodus of employees and customers.

Instead, they create an oppressive culture of political correctness under the false banner of "inclusion and diversity" to achieve the same ends. They tell the world that they value and encourage "different perspectives, styles, thoughts, and ideas" while they punish or intimidate into silence people with "different perspectives, styles, thoughts, and ideas." While Cisco executives would never admit this, their actions reveal this twisted truth: Cisco values homosexual behavior more than honesty, freedom of religion, and freedom of conscience. They claim to be "inclusive and diverse," but their orthodoxy is more closed and narrow than the most rabid fundamentalist church.

Is it the same at your workplace? Are you tired of having to hide your conservative or religious beliefs as if you live in a totalitarian state rather than in America? If you continue to cower in silence before an intolerant militant minority, it will only get worse. To paraphrase Edmund Burke, "All that is necessary for evil to prevail is for good people to do nothing." It's time to do something—speak up.

Sex is the New Religion

Sex is the new religion in America. Notice that most of the cultural wars that divide the country surround issues of sex: abortion, same-sex marriage, government-funded abortion and contraception, and now even what bathrooms we should use!

The adherents of this new religion (it's actually an old religion resurrected) have no tolerance for those who disagree with them. The religion of sex is a religion of the sword. It consists of a determined and vocal minority who bully and cut down Christians and other theists. This clash of orthodoxies has opposing values with moralists on both sides demanding their rights.

One side says, "everyone must celebrate my perceived gender and my same-sex marriage"—a moral position. The other side says, "God or my conscience prevents me from doing so"—also a moral position. Can anyone see any middle ground here? There is none. So the question is, whose moral "right" will take precedence?

The truth is everyone puts limits on marriage—if marriage had no definition it wouldn't be anything. For example, most same-sex marriage proponents *limit* the number in a marriage to two (arbitrarily I might add). So the question isn't whether or not you can limit or define marriage, but where do you limit it? Recognizing that marriage is between a man and a woman is not bigotry, but common sense rooted in the biological facts of nature. That's why the state recognizes marriage to begin with—not because two people love one another but because only heterosexual unions can perpetuate and stabilize society. That is, only heterosexual unions can procreate and best nurture the next generation.

Yet this common sense, natural law truth about marriage is under attack, which is why some states see the need to pass state religious freedom laws. They need to protect the rights of Christians, Muslims, Jews, and anyone else who can't celebrate the orthodoxy of the new religion of sex.

Forget tolerance. This is well beyond tolerance. Now, if you don't agree to *celebrate* same-sex marriage, believers in the religion of sex will commence an inquisition and, without a trial, punish you for heresy. Florists, bakers, photographers, Internet CEOs,[85] and speakers like myself have all discovered that the people who say they are fighting for "tolerance" are often the most intolerant. Those of us who have a diverse view are being excluded in the name of "inclusion and diversity," and even fired and fined because we won't violate our beliefs to satisfy the overbearing clergy of the religion of sex.

Contrary to the media narrative, these laws do not allow businesses to deny anyone service at a retail establishment.

85 Any news search will reveal several examples of Christian business folk being punished—not for refusing to serve homosexuals in retail establishments, but for refusing to participate in same-sex ceremonies. For example, see 3 Common Myths Used Against Christian Bakers like Aaron and Melissa Klein and Jack Phillips. http://www.adflegal.org/detailspages/blog-details/allianceedge/2016/04/07/3-common-myths-used-against-christian-bakers-like-aaron-and-melissa-klein-and-jack-phillips. Even same-sex marriage advocate Andrew Sullivan finds such bullying appalling. See http://dish.andrewsullivan.com/2014/04/03/the-hounding-of-brendan-eich/ (accessed May 10, 2016).

No one is doing that now, and you wouldn't be in business long if you did—the free market would see to it. Moreover, those who actually follow Jesus *want* to be with and serve unbelievers as Jesus did. We just can't *advocate* events or ideas that go against Christ's teaching on marriage (see Matthew 19:4-6).

The truth is *these laws are not swords but shields*. They are intended to *shield* those in the traditional religions from those in the religion of sex who would use the sword of government to *force* the traditionalists—mostly the Christians—to participate in ceremonies that go against their religion or conscience. In other words, the laws are designed to *prevent discrimination* against the traditionalists, not enable them to discriminate against those in the religion of sex.

America has a long history of successfully balancing a variety of religious and moral beliefs with other important interests. Even when military service was involuntary, we still made room for conscientious objectors who did not want to carry weapons. *If we can allow people to exempt themselves from defending the country—the most important responsibility our government has—we can certainly allow people to exempt themselves from performing same-sex wedding ceremonies!*

What compelling government interest is there to force someone to support a same-sex wedding? It's not like there is a shortage of people willing to do them. If a seventy-year-old grandmother (Baronelle Stutzman[86]) can't work your same-sex wedding because she is a Christian, then why not go to

86 Baronelle Stutzman is a florist being sued by the State of Washington because she can't, in good conscience, participate in a same-sex wedding. http://www.cnn.com/2015/02/20/living/stutzman-florist-gay/ (accessed May 10, 2016).

someone else who would be happy to do it? Why don't we ever hear about Christians suing gay business owners for refusing to print up anti-gay marriage fliers? Why is "tolerance" only a one-way street to the religion of sex?

Should a Muslim caterer be forced to do a same-sex wedding? Should a Muslim t-shirt maker be forced to print gay pride t-shirts, or those that satirize Mohammad? The religion of sex would prefer we don't use Muslims in our questions—stick to Christians please.

There is no compelling government interest to force a business to do a wedding or print up anything against their beliefs. That's why the religion of sex is distorting the facts and throwing a temper tantrum to get government to force people to violate their conscience. Their approach reminds me of what bad preachers write in the margin of their sermon notes: "Logic weak here—pound pulpit!" Apparently, the religion of sex just can't tolerate the fact that some people won't accept their false doctrines on faith.

I wish there was a compromise position here but there isn't. We have two opposing values in direct conflict. The religion of sex values the sword of government compulsion over the freedom of religion and conscience. Do you?

On the Wrong Side of History? No, on the Wrong Side of God, Evolution, and Humanity

We've been told that people who want to maintain the man-woman definition of marriage are "on the wrong side of history." Perhaps so. Maybe "history," which is determined largely by how people behave, will continue to move toward making marriage genderless in the 90 percent of governments that still maintain the natural definition.

But remember, Moses was on the wrong side of the golden calf. Lincoln's emancipation proclamation was on the wrong side of *Dred Scott*—the 1857 Supreme Court decision that declared blacks were "so far inferior that they had no rights." Thus, being on the wrong side of some popular moral assertion doesn't necessarily mean that your position is wrong.

Now that five judges say that same-sex marriage is a new "right," I would like to ask a more foundational question. Where do rights come from? Specifically, where does the right to same-sex marriage come from?

If you say that rights come from governments or constitutions, then how can they really be rights? Isn't a right something you have regardless of what a government says? If same-sex marriage is really a right, then you actually possess that right even if you live under a government that doesn't recognize same-sex marriage. You may not be able to exercise it, but you have it nonetheless.

Moreover, if there is no overarching moral standard that transcends human governments, then how could we prosecute Nazi soldiers for violating the rights of others? The Nazis were just following their government.

The truth is that rights don't come from men or governments. Instead, "to secure these rights, Governments are instituted among Men," as our Founders wrote in the

Declaration of Independence. That was the entire point of the Declaration—the government of King George was usurping the rights of colonists, so we declared our independence.

Doesn't evolution provide us with a right to same-sex marriage? Some make this claim but without thinking it through. If natural selection has a goal of survival, then how could same-sex marriage help with that? Such marriages are an agreement to stay in a sterile and medically unhealthy relationship—the exact antithesis of survival. If everyone lived faithfully in same-sex marriage, the human race would end quite quickly.

I don't think macroevolution is true, but even if it is, moral rights don't result from biological processes. Rights are *prescriptive* and come from an authoritative person. Biological processes are *descriptive* and have no authority to tell you what to do. How does a mutating genetic code have the moral authority to tell you how you *ought* to behave or how you *ought* to treat others?

The truth is, just like history describes what does happen and not what *ought* to happen, biology describes what does survive, not what *ought* to survive. Why should humans survive as opposed to anything else? And which humans—we or the Nazis?

Even if one could make the case that evolution somehow makes survival a moral right, we are left with several thorny questions. Isn't self-sacrifice to save others morally superior to your own survival? Should a person murder if it helps him survive? Should a person rape to propagate his DNA? Should a society exterminate the weak and undesirable to improve the gene pool and help the desirable survive? Hitler used evolutionary theory to justify just that. Homosexuals were many of his victims.

So if rights don't come from governments or evolution, then where do they come from? To truly be rights, they can only come from an authoritative being whose nature is the very standard of perfect goodness. That's what we mean by God.

Without God there is no authoritative moral standard beyond humanity, which means that every action or behavior is merely a matter of human opinion. The murder of Jews, gypsies, and homosexuals—it's just your opinion against Hitler's opinion. Child crucifixions—it's just your opinion against that of ISIS. Freedom of speech—that's just your opinion to that of a dictator. Gay bashing is bad—again, just your opinion.

The same holds true with any supposed right, including the right to same-sex marriage. While you can get five judges to assert it is a right, without God it is just an opinion—thus the Court's judgment is aptly named.

But couldn't God approve of same-sex marriage?

The major religious books state just the opposite. So does the Natural Law derived from God's nature. Thomas Jefferson called this "Nature's Law" from which we get "self-evident truths" and the fact that people "are endowed by their Creator with certain unalienable Rights." Same-sex marriage is not one of them. In fact, Jefferson and other politically incorrect Founding Founders called homosexual acts "crimes against nature" because such acts go against the natural design of the body and frustrate the goal of perpetuating humanity. This observation is not based on bigotry but on biology. It's ironic that our Founding Fathers were more apt to follow science than today's secular left who ignore science when they insist that biological gender is changeable and sexual behavior is not. The exact opposite is true!

Since real rights can only come from God (see my new book *Stealing from God: Why Atheists Need God to Make Their Case*), if you want to insist same-sex marriage is a right then you must assume that God is for same-sex marriage. But then you must also assume the implausible notion that God wants you to harm your health and that of the human race by contributing to its extinction. How's that for love? Don't be fruitful. Don't multiply. Don't survive. Same-sex marriage is not only on the wrong side of God and evolution, it's on the wrong side of humanity.

So if not from governments, evolution, or God, where does the "right" to same-sex marriage come from? Our imaginations—perhaps well intended imaginations but imaginations nonetheless.

Should You Do Your Job or Obey Your Conscience?

Should Christians ever disobey their government? Some say no. But Kim Davis sides with Martin Luther King and thinks civil disobedience is justified. Ms. Davis is the Rowan County Kentucky clerk who spent five days in jail for refusing to put her name on same-sex marriage licenses.

Claiming to be a new Christian, Ms. Davis is also a long-time Democrat.

In court, Judge David Bunning told Davis: "The court cannot condone the willful disobedience of its lawfully issued order." He said that "if you give people the opportunity to choose which orders they follow, that's what potentially causes problems."

Judge Bunning is absolutely right. This is the kind of chaos that results when people do not respect the law. But I'm not referring to Kim Davis—I'm referring to the United States Supreme Court. There is no justification in the Constitution for judicially imposing genderless marriage on every state in the union. Five unelected justices simply imposed their own law on 330 million people.

But does that justify civil disobedience? Where do you draw the line?

Certainly, there is a line somewhere. After all, we laud those behind the Underground Railroad who freed slaves and those who protected Jews in Nazi Germany. While bad marriage laws are obviously not as serious, consider a more equivalent scenario. Suppose the Supreme Court decided to drop the age of consent in every state to twelve years old, a position Ruth Bader Ginsberg supported before she became a Supreme Court Justice.[87] Would you think that Kim Davis should be forced to endorse the marriage of a seventy-five-year-old man who brought a twelve-year-old girl into her

---

87 See http://www.nationalreview.com/bench-memos/53898/slates-noah-graham-and-ginsburg-wrong-again-ed-whelan. Accessed May 10, 2016.

office? I hope you can see that there is a line and it's not far from Kim Davis.

Liberals believe in civil disobedience—when it suits their cause. Despite chanting, "Do your job!" outside Kim Davis's office, liberals were rejoicing when San Francisco mayor Gavin Newsom ordered clerks to violate California law and issue marriage licenses to same-sex couples in 2004. They certainly were not chanting "Do your job" outside of Attorney General Eric Holder's office when he told the states last year to ignore their own laws that defined marriage as the union of a man and a woman. And liberals were not asking a federal judge to throw President Obama in jail when he refused to do his job by defending the Defense of Marriage Act in Court.

So just ten minutes ago liberals believed that defying marriage laws was heroic! Now their blatant double standard is all too obvious—they laud civil disobedience when it's used to advance the religion of sex and denounce it when it's used to protect Christian or natural law beliefs.

But on what authority does one defy the government? One man who wanted a same-sex marriage license asked Kim Davis on "what authority" was she not issuing licenses. She cited God.

Yet the question needs to be asked of both sides. By what authority did Newsom, Holder, Obama, and other liberal politicians defy the law? They certainly weren't citing God or the Creator cited in our Declaration of Independence as giving us unalienable rights. Without an authority beyond man's law, there is no authority for their actions nor is there any objective standard to ground unalienable rights. Without God, every right claim is merely a human opinion.[88] At least Kim Davis, agree with her or not, is citing an authority beyond herself.

Civil disobedience has rich precedent in the United States. In fact, our country was founded on it largely to secure religious freedom. Civil disobedience also has precedent in the Bible. When Pharaoh ordered Hebrew midwives to murder all Hebrew boys, they disobeyed and even lied to the authorities (see Exodus 1). Daniel and his friends peacefully defied laws that contradicted God's commands. Likewise, when the Jewish authorities told John and Peter to stop telling people the good news that Jesus paid for your sins and rose from the dead, they disobeyed saying that they would obey God rather than men (see Acts 4).

Therefore, the principle for Christians is this: civil disobedience is necessary when a government compels you to sin or prevents you from doing something God commands you to do. You don't disobey the government merely because it permits others to sin—only when it compels you to do so. Kim Davis thinks that line has been crossed.

It's actually not hard to avoid crossing the line. In North Carolina, we passed a law to allow people like Kim Davis to opt out of endorsing relationships that violated their religious or moral beliefs. Since other government employees are more than happy to issue licenses, no one is inconvenienced or forced to violate conscience. We do this for far

88 See Frank Turek, *Stealing from God: Why Atheists Need God to Make Their Case*, NavPress, 2015.

more serious issues than weddings. Even during a time of war when we draft people to defend the country, we allow for conscientious objectors to opt out. If we can allow exemptions for government employees involved in protecting the very existence of our nation, we can certainly allow exemptions for government employees involved in weddings!

Will the Kentucky legislature act to pass such a law? Unfortunately, I doubt the activists who are always demanding tolerance will tolerate such reasonableness. It seems that some people just can't live and let live. They will not rest until all opposition is crushed and everyone is forced to celebrate what they are doing.

If that's your position, I have a question for you: Why would you want anyone who disagrees with your wedding to have anything to do with it? Go to another clerk, another florist, another photographer. Why force people to violate their conscience when there are so many other people willing to help you and celebrate with you? After all, isn't this supposed to be a time when "love wins?

Apparently not. For some liberals, "love wins" as long as everyone agrees with them. Those that disagree will not like the kind of "love" some liberals dish out. Are the same people chanting "love wins" some of the same people who issued death threats to Kim Davis? It certainly wasn't the Christians.

The truth is, Kim Davis and other victims of "tolerance" don't want a holy war. Davis just doesn't want her signature on the license. She suggested other government officials sign, and Judge Bunning finally agreed, but a law needs to be passed to prevent future problems.

North Carolina has led the way. It remains to be seen if liberals in Kentucky will accept that way. If their recent history is a guide, I'm afraid they will demand that every knee bow and every tongue confess the dogma of their secular religion.

The Bathroom Wars: Can Bruce Springsteen Refuse to Play a Gay Wedding?

I agree with Bruce Springsteen who cancelled his concert in my adopted home state of North Carolina because he objected to HB2 (the bathroom law). I also agree with Paypal, which cancelled their plans to expand in Charlotte because they think the law is "discriminatory." Why? Because I believe that performers and businesses have every right not to do business with those whom they disagree. In other words, they have the right to discriminate against the people of North Carolina.

But if liberals can deny services to people with whom they disagree, then why can't the conservatives?

When Bruce Springsteen refuses to do a concert in North Carolina for moral reasons, he's a hero to the liberals and the media, which are the same thing. Yet when a conservative band, florist, or photographer refuses to work at a gay wedding for moral or religious reasons, the left and the media bully those folks mercilessly as intolerant bigots. They do so while claiming to be against bullying and for "tolerance." If it weren't for double standards, liberals would have no standards!

In America, a gay t-shirt maker should not be forced to print up anti-gay marriage t-shirts. A Christian or Muslim photographer should not be forced to photograph a gay wedding. If Bruce has the right to deny service, so does everyone.

Of course HB2 has nothing to do with denying services to anyone. It's about public heath and safety. All good laws discriminate, but they discriminate against *behaviors* not people. Bathroom use is a behavior, and keeping men out of women's restrooms and showers is a public safety law that rightly discriminates against the behavior of a man going into a women's restroom or shower. It discriminates against that behavior, but it doesn't discriminate against people.

If any law is wrongly discriminatory, it is the bad law passed by the Charlotte City Council that created this controversy. The Charlotte City Council law actually discriminated against women and children by making public restrooms unsafe for them. The ACLU has already filed a lawsuit alleging HB2 does not provide "equal protection" to some folks. Ironically, it's only because of HB2 that women and children get "equal protection" from *heterosexual* predators in public bathrooms!

There are 21,054 convicted sex offenders in North Carolina—one of them was a leader in getting the Charlotte ordinance to pass that created the need for HB2 in the first place—a fact conveniently ignored by the mainstream media. Is it bigotry to protect women and children from these people? No, it's loving and right. We shouldn't put millions of women and children at risk of *heterosexual* predators (the threat is not from the transgendered) who use the law as a ruse to gain access to women's restrooms and showers.[89] We don't endanger millions to make one or two out of every thousand feel better about what bathroom they use. If one guy is blind, we don't endanger everyone by forcing them to wear blindfolds so the blind guy feels better.

George Orwell said, "In a time of universal deceit, telling the truth is a revolutionary act." When you tell the truth about homosexuality today, you can be sure that the central tools of deceit—name-calling and bullying—will be unleashed. That's what the misnamed Human's Rights Campaign does. They smear conservatives as "bigots" in order to bully them out of the debate and even out of their jobs. In America today, it's much easier to win with demagoguery than evidence. If you convince the majority that your opponents are "bigots," then you automatically win even if you're the bully actually practicing bigotry.

Opposition to harmful behavior is not bigotry—it's wise. In fact, to really *love* people, we often have to *oppose* what they do! A mom is certainly not loving if she doesn't oppose behaviors that will harm her child.

Unfortunately, some on the left and in business falsely equate opposition to a behavior as prejudice toward people who engage in that behavior. That's the central fallacy in virtually every argument the misnamed Human Rights Campaign puts out. If you don't agree with every aspect of LGBT behavior or their political goals, you are somehow bigoted against people who identify that way. If political

---

89 Sexual predators have already done this on several occasions in jurisdictions with such laws. See the video referenced in http://townhall.com/columnists/frankturek/2016/03/30/six-reasons-north-carolina-got-it-right-n2141010 (accessed May 10, 2016); search for "Women: Decide for yourselves" on YouTube. Or go here: https://www.youtube.com/watch?v=uzwMJAFWLtQ&feature=youtu.be

opposition is bigotry, then the activists at the Human Rights Campaign are bigots for opposing conservatives. In fact, if anything is bigoted, it's the failure to read HB2, mischaracterize it, and then to blindly goose-step to the propaganda put out by the misnamed Human Rights Campaign.

The truth is conservatives have good reasons based in public health and safety for not wanting to advocate same-sex marriage or men in women's bathrooms. But it's much easier for the Human Rights Campaign to ignore those arguments and call people names.

The misnamed Human Rights Campaign wants LGBT preferences to supersede everyone else's rights. According to them, the only right you have is to agree with them. That's why they think someone like Bruce Springsteen has rights that you don't have.

Feelings vs. Facts: Should "sexual orientation" be a protected class?

Should sexual orientation be a protected class? Some will say yes because race is, but the comparison doesn't work. Race is not a behavior and it has no impact on your behavior. LGBT issues are all about advancing behaviors that violate the deeply held moral and religious beliefs of many Americans. And LGBT political goals are all about imposing certain objectionable behaviors on others, whether it's forcing participation in a gay wedding or allowing men into women's bathrooms and showers.

LGBT political goals often involve a solution looking for a problem. Are LGBT people having trouble getting work? The median income of LGBT households is significantly higher than the average American household ($61,000 vs. $50,000).[90]

Are LGBT people being discriminated against in the workplace because of their sexual behaviors off the job? To the contrary—they often run the workplace and are favored in the workplace!

Why else would so many companies immediately express outrage over a commonsense law (HB2) to keep men out of women's bathrooms and showers? (By the way, these are the same companies that are doing business with countries that kill homosexuals.) When HB2 was passed, the companies complaining hadn't mandated gender neutral bathrooms in their own workplaces, but they were upset when the government refused to mandate them on everyone. Why were they upset? Because despite the irrationality and hypocrisy of it all, HR departments in corporate America are in the pocket of the LGBT movement.

Ask anyone in corporate America this question: Are you more likely to experience problems at work for supporting same-sex marriage or opposing it? It's not even close. If any group is being discriminated against in corporate America, it is Christians hiding under their desks for fear of being outed and then excluded by the "inclusion and diversity" police.

---

90 For more on sexual orientation laws and the issue of same-sex marriage, see Ryan Anderson's excellent book, *Truth Overruled: The Future of Marriage and Religious Freedom*, Regnery, 2015. This statistic is found on page 130.

When Cisco and Bank of America fired me because I had written this book, I personally agreed that they had the right to fire me. I know there are religious protections that apply to employees (I was a consultant). But regardless of any legal protections, I personally believe that if you are in the private sector and don't want to work with me because of my beliefs, fine—I don't have a right to your job. Just please don't call yourself "inclusive and diverse." That's fraud. And keep in mind that consumers may express their disagreement with your treatment of conscientious objectors by boycotting your business.

I think we should keep the government out of the workplace as much as possible. Using the strong arm of government to make "sexual orientation" a protected class would actually make the workplace less fair because it would result in employment *preference* for people with a long list of sexual feelings and behaviors.

Someone who claimed a homosexual orientation—or someone who chooses the *behavior* of cross-dressing at work, for example—would have more job security than John or Jane Doe. How so? Because if a company has to downsize, who are they going to let go—one of the helpless Does or the person who can bring a financially devastating lawsuit alleging "discrimination"?

Moreover, there isn't any medical consensus as to what sexual orientation or transgenderism is. Where should the line be drawn? Should businesses be forced to give *preference* to those who identify as "ambigender; bigender; blurgender; collgender; conflictgender; cosmicgender; crystagender; deliciagender; duragender; demiflux; domgender;

fissgender; gemelgender; gendercluster; genderfluid; gendersea; genderfuzz; genderfractal; genderspiral; genderswirl; gendervex; gyaragender; libragender; ogligender; pangender; polygender; and trigender"? These are all taken from a transgender website. How does it make sense to give *preference* to people who have a mismatch between their psychology and their biology?[91]

Facebook has been praised by the LGBT community for allowing more than fifty sexual "identities," and they have added a "custom" option. Get ready for complete workplace chaos if these feelings get legal preference over the biological facts and John and Jane Doe.

Workplace laws should be based on facts, not feelings. Your biological sex is a fact, but your sexual orientation is a feeling, regardless of its cause. If laws are based on feelings, then:

- If you feel like a sixty-five-year-old Army veteran, do you have a legal right to an Army pension and social security?
- If you're white but feel black, do you have a legal right to get preference from the government for being a minority owned business?

91 Dr. Paul McHugh of Johns Hopkins University points out that transgenderism is a mental disorder on par with anorexia. With anorexia, a dangerously underweight person falsely believes that they are overweight. In transgenderism, a physical male or female falsely believes to be the other sex. McHugh reveals that Hopkins stopped doing "gender reassignment" surgery because patients were still so troubled *after the surgery* that they had a suicide rate twenty times higher than the rest of the population. Dr. McHugh, who is a psychiatrist, ended his article in the *Wall Street Journal* this way: "'Sex change' is biologically impossible. People who undergo sex-reassignment surgery do not change from men to women or vice versa. Rather, they become feminized men or masculinized women. Claiming that this is civil-rights matter and encouraging surgical intervention is in reality to collaborate with and promote a mental disorder." See http://www.wsj.com/articles/paul-mchugh-transgender-surgery-isnt-the-solution-1402615120. Accessed May 26, 2016.

- If you feel like you're born with an anti-gay gene, is the government discriminating against you by forcing you to abide by gay rights laws? After all, if you're born with the anti-gay gene, don't you have a legal right to live out your orientation?

By LGBT logic, your feelings should provide you with those rights. If the feeling we call "sexual orientation" must be protected, then why aren't we stuck giving *preference* to all sorts of harmful sexual behaviors including pedophilia, bestiality, polygamy, and adultery?

Some will say because those are harmful behaviors, but as we have seen, homosexual behavior is also medically harmful. True, these behaviors are not all equally harmful, but the logic used to justify them—feelings or "sexual orientation"—is the same. In other words, if you want to justify giving preference to particular behaviors, you have to use another argument than people having certain feelings because the logic behind the argument results in absurd conclusions.

As we've already seen, the "born that way" argument doesn't help the case either. The truth is *all* of us were born with an "orientation" to bad behavior, but those desires don't justify the behaviors. They certainly don't justify using the strong arm of government to force others to *prefer* those behaviors in the workplace or elsewhere.

Again, this is different than race. While race protections and affirmative action unfortunately create reverse discrimination by giving preference to certain people, race has no impact on behavior or business results. But cross-dressing, for example, is a choice to behave in a way that can hinder job performance and drive off customers and profits. A business owner should not be legally forced to suffer because an employee engages in behavior that hurts business.

So when people ask me, "Should people be fired just because they have a certain sexual orientation?" My answer is no, unless of course it results in behaviors that directly hurt an employee's job performance. Making sexual orientation a protected class won't fix existing workplace problems (LGBT folks are doing quite well), and it would create a far worse problem—*reverse discrimination* against more than 96 percent of the population. That's anything but "equality."

Why Christians Should Be in Politics

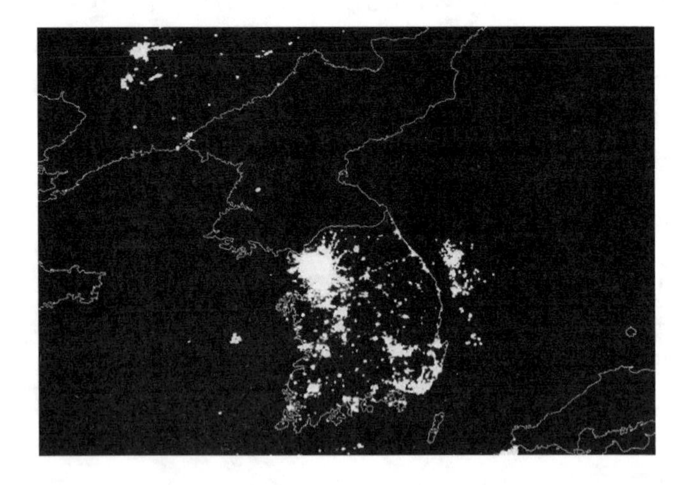

When I hear Christians saying we ought not to get involved in politics but just "preach the Gospel," I show them this satellite picture of the Korean peninsula. Here we see a homogenous population of mostly Koreans separated by a well-fortified border. South Korea is full of freedom, food, and productivity—it's one of the most Christianized countries in the world. North Korea is a concentration camp. They have no freedom, no food, and little Christianity.

What's the primary reason for the stark difference between these two countries? Politics. The South politically allows freedom while the North does not.

Ironically, Christians who shun politics to supposedly advance the Gospel are actually allowing others to *stop* the Gospel. How so? Because *politics and law affect one's ability to preach the Gospel!* If you think otherwise, visit some of the countries I have visited—Iran, Saudi Arabia, and China. You cannot legally "preach the Gospel" in those countries—or practice other aspects of your religion freely—because politically they've ruled it out, as they have in North Korea.

Politics affect virtually every area of your life through the laws made by government. So if you care about your family, business, church, school, children, money, property, home, security, healthcare, safety, freedom, and your ability to "preach the Gospel," then you should care about politics.

Leaders throughout the Bible—including Joseph, Moses, Daniel, Nehemiah, Mordecai, Esther, John the Baptist, and Paul—"went political" to influence civil governments to govern morally. Even Jesus Himself got involved in politics when He publically chastised the Pharisees—the religious and *political* leaders of Israel—for neglecting "the more important matters of the law."

Unfortunately, our lawmakers today are doing the same thing. They use the force of law to tell us what light bulbs to use and what the school lunch menu should be, but they neglect to put restrictions on the taking of human life by abortion! What could be more important than life? The right to life is the right to all other rights. If you don't have life, you don't have anything.

What can Christians do? We can't legislate morality, can we? News flash: *All laws legislate morality!* Morality is about right and wrong, and all laws declare one behavior right and the opposite behavior wrong. So the question is not whether we can legislate morality, but whose morality will we legislate?

The answer our Founding Fathers gave was the "self-evident" morality given to us by our Creator—the same moral law the Apostle Paul said that all people have "written on their hearts." In other words, not *my* morality or *your* morality, but *the* morality—the one we inherited, not the one we invented. This doesn't mean that every moral or political issue has clear right and wrong answers. It only means that "the more important matters of the law"—life, marriage, and religious freedom for example—*do* have clear answers that we should heed.

Notice that our Founders did not have to establish a particular denomination or force religious practice in order to legislate a moral code. Our country justifies moral rights with theism, but does not require its citizens to acknowledge or practice theism. That's why liberals are wrong when they charge that Christians are trying to impose a "theocracy" or violate the "separation of church and state." They fail to distinguish between religion and morality.

Broadly defined, religion involves our duty to God while morality involves our duty to one another. Our lawmakers are not telling people how, when, or if to go to church—that would be legislating religion—but lawmakers cannot avoid telling people how they should treat one another. That is legislating morality and that is what all laws do.

Opposition to abortion or same-sex marriage, for example, does not entail the establishment of a "theocracy." Churches and the Bible also teach that murder, theft, and child abuse are wrong, but no one says laws prohibiting such acts establish a theocracy or are a violation of the "separation of church and state." If the government could not pass laws consistent with church or biblical teachings, then all criminal laws would have to be overturned because they are all in some way consistent with at least one of the Ten Commandments.

Second, there are churches on both sides of these issues. Some liberal churches, contrary to Scripture, actually *support* abortion and same-sex marriage. So if church supported positions could not be put into law, then we could not have laws either way on abortion or same-sex marriage. Absurd.

Finally, most proponents of same-sex marriage argue as if they have some kind of moral right to having their relationships endorsed by the state. They claim that they don't have "equal rights" or that they are being "discriminated" against. Likewise, abortion advocates claim they have a moral "right" to choose an abortion. None of these claims are true, as we have seen. Nevertheless, their arguments, while flawed, expose the fact that independent of religion, they seek to legislate *their* morality rather than *the* morality.

If you have a problem with *the* morality, don't blame me. I didn't make it up. I didn't make up the fact that abortion is wrong, that men are not designed for other men, or that natural marriage is the foundation of a civilized society. Those unchangeable objective truths about reality are examples of the "Laws of Nature" from "Nature's God," as the Declaration of Independence puts it. We only hurt others and ourselves by suppressing those truths and legislating immoral laws.

When we fail to legislate morally, others impose immorality. For example, with the judicial mandate of same-sex marriage, totalitarian political correctness is overriding the religious liberties of businesses, charities, and even parents. Same-sex marriage prevents you from running your business, educating your children, or practicing your religion in accord with your conscience. Soon you may not be able to merely speak biblically about homosexual behavior, as is the case in Canada. This is because those who say they are fighting for "tolerance" are often the most intolerant.

Unless Christians begin to influence politics and the culture more significantly, we will continue to lose the very freedoms that enable us to live according to our beliefs and spread the Gospel all over the world. That's why you should not vote for candidates merely because of their race or religion, but because they will govern morally on the more important matters of the law—life, marriage, and religious freedom.

Our country has a choice to make: either maintain the value of freedom enshrined in our Constitution or usurp the value of freedom by mandating conformity to the LGBT agenda. Unless the church and other freedom loving people begin to speak up and get involved—and by that I mean in politics, education, the media, and law—we will lose the very freedoms our Founders spilled their blood to secure.

Oh, one more thing. If you are a pastor worried about your tax-exempt status:

1. You have more freedom than you think to speak on political and moral issues from the pulpit.[92]
2. If you do not speak up for truth now, you will soon lose your freedom to speak for anything, including the Gospel.
3. You are called to be salt and light, not tax exempt.

92 Go here to learn about your rights: http://www.adflegal.org/issues/religious-freedom/church

PART VI

Hard Facts about the Transgender Craze

Does Love Require Approval?

A few years ago, Dr. Michael Brown and I debated two representatives of the LGBTQ community on whether love requires us to approve or affirm a loved one's position. We picked this topic because many people today believe that love requires approval: if you love me, you will approve of what I want to do. Dr. Brown and I argued that love does not require approval; our opponents argued that it does.

At one point in the debate, we asked the other side, "Do you love us?" They said, "Yes." We then asked, "Do you approve of our position?" They said, "No." We then pointed out that they had just lost the debate because they didn't approve of our position but still claimed to love us.[93]

Love does not require approval. Everyone knows this upon reflection. If your parents approved of everything you

93 Video of the debate: www.youtube.com/watch?v=m5Etn0_z_1s&t=1227s.

wanted to do as a kid, would your parents have been loving? No, they would have been unloving. Loving people means seeking what is best for them, and that means standing in the way of behaviors that will hurt them or others.

Too often we shy away from this tough love because we want to protect ourselves from blowback. We would rather allow people to remain on the path of self-destruction than to see them upset with us. The brilliant Thomas Sowell put it this way, "When you want to help people, you tell them the truth. When you want to help yourself, you tell them what they want to hear."

When we think of LGBTQ issues, we often think about our friends and relatives who consider themselves part of that community. Out of our love for them we may be inclined to tell them what they want to hear, to approve and celebrate all things LGBTQ. However, that inclination may lead us to take unloving positions. That seems to be happening now. In our efforts to be loving and tolerant, we now seem unable to defend any moral lines, including those that protect children.

How did we get to the point that a fifteen-year-old girl was allowed to have her perfectly healthy breasts removed in the State of Oregon without parental consent? Or that a thirteen-year-old girl was allowed to take puberty blockers in the State of Washington without parental consent—blockers that would likely make her infertile for life? Or why did the Biden administration signal in 2022 that it was willing to take children as young as three years old from parents who disagreed with their "gender-affirming care" (more on this later)? Because we have lost the courage or will to say "No" after saying "Yes" for so long.

In case you have not noticed, the culture war over sex did not end when the Supreme Court mandated same-sex marriage on the entire nation. After that, I had hoped there would be a period of peace in the sexual culture war. After all, the Left received the huge social and political affirmation they wanted. They should have been content, right?

I had hoped so, but instead they escalated their efforts to obliterate more sexual boundaries, particularly the biological boundaries that define men and women. Suddenly, biology itself was discarded in the name of "civil rights" for transgender people.

According to our government and many activists, this new civil right must be imposed on children as young as three. Anyone who disagrees or holds a diverse viewpoint will not be tolerated and will instead be excluded from polite society—ironically in the name of "inclusion, tolerance, and diversity." The logic behind this new movement is apparently so weak that if anyone questions it, their freedoms of speech and religion must be sacrificed.

People argue over why this movement is happening. Some claim this effort to destroy sexual boundaries and the nuclear family is part of a larger Leftist agenda to destroy Western civilization. Why this movement is happening is controversial. *That* it's happening is undeniable.

Why the Rise in Transgenderism?

Just how prevalent is transgenderism? By its prominence in our public discourse, you would think half the population has declared themselves trans. However, gender dysphoria has been a rare condition historically. Until recently, it affected only about 1 out of every 10,000 people, most of them biological boys thinking they were girls. In fact, prior to 2012, there was no scientific literature showing that gender dysphoria even affected teenage girls.[94]

However, over the past decade, there has been a dramatic increase in girls claiming they are really boys. For example, in the U.K. there has been a 4,400 percent increase in girls seeking treatment at gender clinics.[95] Dr. Lisa Littman, a former researcher at Brown University, has termed this "Rapid Onset Gender Dysphoria" (ROGD)—a phenomenon in which children, having displayed no signs of gender dysphoria, suddenly felt it acutely upon puberty. Dr. Littman's research suggests that the primary causal factor in ROGD among girls is an increase in their social media use, especially when they have friends who identify as trans.[96]

Are there other reasons for such a dramatic, overnight increase in trans identification? Women have not experienced significant biological changes in the past decade. In fact, there is no known biological cause for transgenderism in general, much less ROGD.[97] Instead, ROGD appears to be a social contagion transmitted through and exasperated by social media.

94 Abigail Shrier, "Gender Ideology Run Amok," *Imprimis* (June/July 2021): imprimis.hillsdale.edu/gender-ideology-run-amok.

95 Ibid., Shrier.

96 Littman L (2018), "Parent reports of adolescents and young adults perceived to show signs of a rapid onset of gender dysphoria," *PLoS ONE 13(8): e0202330: doi.org/10.1371/journal.pone.0202330.*

97 See "False Assumptions Behind Youth Gender Transitions" by The Society for Evidence Based Gender Medicine (December 30, 2022): segm.org/false-assumptions-gender-affirmation-minors.

Social media has a powerful influence on young people finding their way in life. What do most young people want as they're finding their way? They want to fit in, to be accepted, and to be applauded by their friends. What is the fastest way to do that in today's social media culture? Claim you are trans. Everyone will applaud you. And anyone who suggests this might be harmful will be shouted down as a "bigot" and probably canceled. So, it's no mystery, when teenagers who live on their cellphones feel the angst of puberty, some will be enticed into claiming they are trans—and maybe even transition—thinking it will bring them the peace and approval they crave.

Abigail Shrier, who wrote the seminal book *Irreversible Damage: The Transgender Craze Seducing Our Daughters*, said she has spoken to families at top girls' schools "who attest that 15, 20, or in one case 30 percent of the girls in their daughter's seventh grade class identify as trans. When you see figures like that, you're witnessing a social contagion in action. There is no other reasonable explanation."[98]

Please understand, I am *not* saying everyone who claims to be trans does so because of social media. There are people with true gender dysphoria, which, as we will soon see, has its origin in mental health issues that are often triggered by childhood trauma. What I *am* saying is social media appears to be the main factor in the meteoric rise of young people claiming to be trans.

What's the solution? The good news is that social media is an environment that, with some effort, can be avoided.

98 Abigail Shrier, "Gender Ideology Run Amok," *Imprimis* (June/July 2021): imprimis.hillsdale.edu/gender-ideology-run-amok.

So, if you or someone you know is suddenly struggling with this, there is hope. The next several chapters make the case that transitioning, however well intended, is not the solution to the problems people are experiencing.

Why "Following Your Heart" is Not a Reliable Guide

Although the transgender craze is fueled by social media, it would not have arisen in the first place without the growing identity crisis that many in our culture feel. We modern people are often unsure of our identity. We used to look *up* to God for our identity. However, as society has become more secular, we now tend to look *within* ourselves to discover our authentic identity or "authentic self."

"Follow your feelings; follow your heart to find your authentic self," we are told. If our "authentic self" is culturally popular, we will often look to social media for applause and confirmation for our identity choice.[99] But there are at least four reasons why "following your heart" is usually very bad advice.

First, our hearts are selfish. Take a minute and just ask yourself: Is it easier to be bad or good? Do you have to work at being selfish or selfless? You don't have to teach a two-year-old to say, "Mine!" You have to teach a two-year-old to share. Why? Because human nature is selfish from birth. Following a selfish heart may lead to short-term advantages but long-term disasters, especially in relationships.

---

99 Pastor Tim Keller points out that we may think we are following our hearts, but we are more following our culture. We follow our culture by elevating one heart's desire approved by our culture, while at the same time suppressing another heart's desire that is disapproved by our culture. For more on this, see Tim Keller, "Our Identity: The Christian Alternative to Late Modernity's Story" (11/11/2015): www.youtube.com/watch?v=Ehw87PqTwKw.

Who wants to be in relationships with people who only care about themselves?

Second, our hearts are deceptive. They deceive us into thinking we must have something and have it now. However, when we blindly pursue selfish impulses, we destroy our most important relationships and risk becoming addicted, broken, and alone.

A third reason "following your heart" is poor advice is that it is impossible to do when your heart is conflicted, which is most of the time. Notice that we often have two hearts warring within us.

We want that shiny new car, but we don't want the debt. We want to get married, but we still want to be "free to play the field." We want to have children, but we don't want the responsibility. We want to be fit and healthy, but that box of glazed donuts is sure tempting. A few of us may even want to attempt transitioning to the opposite sex, but we don't want to subject ourselves to the hellish drugs, surgeries, and health complications that accompany it (more on this later). Which *heart* will you follow?

Since we are often conflicted, the road to happiness requires us to say "No" to many heart desires. C.S. Lewis put it brilliantly: "Surrender to all our desires obviously leads to impotence, disease, jealousies, lies, concealment, and everything that is the reverse of health, good humor, and frankness. For any happiness, even in this world, quite a lot of restraint is going to be necessary."[100]

---

100 C. S. Lewis, *Mere Christianity* (Macmillan: 1952), p. 93.

Lewis is spot on. Our hearts do not always point to what is best for us, or even what is "halfway decent" for that matter. We can do much harm to ourselves and others by "following our hearts." If we do so without wisdom and moral restraint, we will by nature act in selfish, destructive ways.

Finally, we can't consistently follow our hearts because our hearts change. Do you have all the same desires you had twenty years ago? Ten years ago? How about five years ago? Not completely, because our hearts change and grow.

This is especially true of young people. Kids go through phases. It is a part of growing up. Just because a child feels out of place in their own body is no reason to reach for hormones and a scalpel. What kid does *not* feel uncomfortable or awkward in their body as they go through adolescence? That's a natural part of puberty.

Most young people who claim to be trans also have changes of heart. About 80% of young teens who experience gender dysphoria grow out of it by the time they are eighteen.[101] Maturity does that. So, why would anyone block nature's remedy to a problem and castrate or sterilize a child for a feeling that is likely to soon change on its own? One puberty blocker now given to children is Lupron, which was once used to chemically castrate sex offenders!

Real Time host Bill Maher, who is not a conservative, spoke some sense into this rush to transition children. He

101 According to studies complied by the Society for Evidence Based Gender Medicine, "Childhood-onset gender dysphoria has been shown to have a high rate of natural resolution, with 61%-98% of children reidentifying with their biological sex during puberty." See SEGM.org. The 80% figure is an average also cited by Dr. Paul McHugh in *Wall Street Journal*: www.wsj.com/articles/paul-mchugh-transgender-surgery-isnt-the-solution-1402615120.

rightfully pointed out how children claiming to be trans is "trendy," and how teenagers will do anything to get "likes" or "stick it to their parents." The hearts of children are constantly changing as they go through "phases" growing up. He quipped, "If kids knew what they wanted to be at age eight, the world would be filled with cowboys and princesses!" Maher then recalled that when he was a kid, he wanted to be a pirate. He said, "Thank God no one took me seriously and scheduled me for eye removal and pegleg surgery!"[102]

Instead of "following your heart," the better, more time-tested advice comes from three thousand years ago. King Solomon of Israel, a man who had everything, was nearly led to despair by blindly following his heart. He wrote this urgent proverb to save us from our own bad choices: **"Guard your heart above all else, for it determines the course of your life" (Proverbs 4:23 NLT).**

"*Guard* your heart above all else." Notice he did not say, "Follow your heart"! If you follow your heart without restraint, you will ruin your relationships and torpedo your life. Instead, *guard* your heart by seeking wisdom from God and wise people you can trust. Otherwise, your selfish, deceptive, conflicting, and changing heart will take you down the wrong path. It may not seem that way initially, but you probably won't like how your story ends. That's why Solomon also warned us, **"There is a way that seems right to a person, but in the end it leads to death" (Proverbs 14:12).**

John Mark Comer put it well: "Giving in to the desires of our flesh does not lead us to freedom and life, as many

102 "New Rule: Along for the Pride" (May 20, 2022): www.youtube.com/watch?v=mMBzfUj5zsg.

people assume, but instead to slavery and, in the worst-case scenario, addiction, which is a kind of prolonged suicide by pleasure."[103]

In the next few chapters, we will see some of the big problems with transitioning and transgender ideology. Following your heart on this issue is fraught with danger. Everyone should know the facts before considering such a life-altering decision.

Five Flaws in Transgender Ideology

Personally, I think most people who support transgenderism for adults (not kids) are well-intended. They realize people suffer with true gender dysphoria and only want what is best for them. I do not doubt their sincere desire to help people live full and prosperous lives. I just think there are fatal flaws in their positions that lead to unintended consequences. Intentions are important, but not at the expense of logic, ethics, and results.

Here are five of those flaws.

Contrary to transgender ideology:

1. The Design of the Body Proves There are Only Two Genders

Transgender advocates insist that gender and sex are independent of each other. Sex is biological, but gender

103 See John Mark Comer, *Live No Lies*, (Waterbook: 2021).

is whatever you determine it to be (and the current list of options seems endless). *That* is what creates gender dysphoria.

Gender and sex were used synonymously from the Stone Age until about ten minutes ago. However, even if you accept that rather recent distinction, it does nothing to advance the transgender case. What people think about themselves does not change the facts about their biology.

The natural design of the human body shows there are only two genders. Humans can either produce sperm or eggs. There is no third reproductive output in humans or mammals. Of course, there are humans who cannot produce either due to biological deficiencies, but that is an *in*capacity, not a *third* capacity to produce something else. Thus, the claim that there are more than two genders is not based on the objective design of biology but on subjective mental states.

People relying on subjective mental states can (and do) invent, claim, and express any gender they want, but that does not mean such genders truly exist. Nor does it mean the rest of society should pretend they exist. Gender expression may be different from gender reality, but nature has only designed two genders.

Those who suffer from gender dysphoria implicitly admit nature's design when they insist that they should be the opposite sex ("should" implies things ought to be different which assumes design). They think they were born in the wrong body. Clearly, something has gone wrong. Either the design of their body or their mind has in some way gone awry.

The question is, how do we fix that? We will address it below.

2. Transgenderism Must Presuppose Fixed Genders

While transgender advocates deny that there are only two genders, they must unwittingly presuppose two genders for transgenderism to be possible. For example, if I'm a biological man but think I'm a woman, I must have some idea of what a man and woman are to recognize my problem. I must also know what a man and woman are to make the so-called "transition." If genders are completely fluid with no fixed reference points, there would be no way to recognize the mismatch between my biology and psychology and no destination of my transition. In other words, "gender dysphoria" could not exist without two known, fixed genders.

The denial of fixed genders has sparked a bit of a civil war among some in the LGBTQ community, because if the T's get their way, the Ls, Gs, and Bs don't exist. How can one be lesbian, gay, or bisexual if there are no fixed genders? Each of those identities rely on fixed genders. Likewise, some feminists are unhappy because, without fixed genders, there are no women and therefore no women's rights.[104]

This is one reason Matt Walsh's documentary, "What is a Woman?," has so many transgender advocates and Leftwing academics stumped by the question, "What is a woman?" They are caught in a dilemma. If they say a woman is a

104 Harry Potter author, J.K. Rowling, is one who has made the point that transgender ideology erases women and the gains made by women. She has stood strong against the online mob who ignores her arguments and mindlessly charges her with being "transphobic." Calling people names instead of addressing their arguments is a logical fallacy and prevents people from learning and making progress.

biological female, then transgender ideology is false. If they refuse to define a woman, transgenderism is not possible. Who is transitioning to what? And what happened to women's rights?

That is why many responded to Matt's persistent question with the circular non-answer, "A woman is anyone who identifies as a woman." But what is a woman?

As recently as December 2022, the Cambridge Dictionary bowed to the woke mob by offering an updated definition for the words "man" and "woman." Though "woman" is still primarily defined as an "adult female human being," a secondary definition has been added to accommodate adults "who live and/or identify as female though may have been said to have a different sex at birth."[105]

3. You Can Change Your Mind But Not Your Biology

If our biology and psychology are mismatched, or if something has gone wrong with our design, why do we think changing our biology instead of our mind is the way to fix the problem? We don't do this for other conditions.

When anorexics falsely think they are overweight, we don't say, "You're right. Let me get you some liposuction." For people who honestly believe they should have healthy limbs cut off, a condition known as "trans-abled", we don't say, "You know, you're right. If you think you should not

---

105 Harmeet Kaur, "Cambridge Dictionary's definitions for 'man' and 'woman' now include trans people," CNN (December 15, 2022): www.cnn.com/2022/12/15/us/cambridge-dictionary-woman-definition-trans-cec.

have a right arm, we will cut if off for you." So, why do we think we should cut off perfectly healthy sex organs? In every parallel case, we treat people with mental dysphoria with psychiatry, not surgery. That is the right and compassionate thing to do.

Why? Because while you can change your mind, it is literally impossible to change your biology. As unpopular as that may sound to some, it is a scientific fact that you cannot change your biology. No matter what you do to alter or remove your sexual organs, you cannot change your DNA or the many thousands of biological differences between men and women.[106]

Any attempt to "transition" between the sexes implicitly admits these differences and affirms the binary nature of gender. Otherwise, there would be no use for hormones or puberty blockers. In fact, if there were no differences in the physical and biological designs of men and women, transgenderism would not only be impossible but unnecessary. If men and women were the same, there would be no desire to transition.

While some people certainly feel that they are in the wrong body, the truth is, no biological male has ever experienced being a biological female or vice versa. It's impossible for them to know personally whether their feelings correspond with that of the opposite sex. As we will soon see, when people feel uncomfortable with their biology, surgery or cross-sex hormones is not the answer.

---

106 See, for example, Cecile Borkhataria,"The REAL difference between men and women: Researchers find 6,500 genes differ between the sexes," *DailyMail.com* (May 4, 2017): www.dailymail.co.uk/sciencetech/article-4475252/There-6-500-genetic-differences-men-women.html.

4. Sex is not "Assigned" at Birth

One way to make people believe something they would not normally believe is to use deceptive language. For example, abortion supporters like to use pleasant-sounding words like "choice," "reproductive rights," or "product of conception" rather than referring to what they are really choosing—the "death of a baby." If you use deceptive language long enough, people will eventually believe it.

Transgender advocates do the same. For transgender ideology to succeed, people must believe that gender is arbitrary and can be chosen. The concept of "gender" must be detached from one's biology or "sex," which is fixed, to accommodate the arbitrary choosing or discovery of one's gender later. That is why transgender advocates work overtime to try and change definitions. Not only do they insist on everyone declaring their pronouns, but they also declare that sex is "assigned" at birth. Everyone knows that sex is not "assigned" at birth but *discovered* at birth or sometimes before. It's not like people vote at gender-reveal parties, or that doctors arbitrarily decide the sex of a newborn. No, they discover and state the baby's sex because there is no ambiguity.

In the extremely rare cases where genitals are ambiguous (intersex), tests are done and choices are made to correct the problem.[107] Most patients end up male or female rather than assuming a non-binary status. This is not the same as transgenderism where people with fully

---

107 Although some have suggested that 1.7% of all births are intersex, the real figure is almost 100 times lower than that at 0.018%. See Sax L. "How common is intersex? a response to Anne Fausto-Sterling," J Sex Res. 2002 Aug;39(3):174-8. doi: 10.1080/00224490209552139. PMID: 12476264: pubmed.ncbi.nlm.nih.gov/12476264.

formed and healthy sexual organs attempt to transition to the opposite sex. Intersex is a biological condition; gender dysphoria is a psychological condition. The existence of intersex conditions does nothing to support the claim that sex is "assigned" at birth. Birth defects do not disprove the norm. In fact, they would be impossible to identify without the norm.[108]

We live in a fallen world. All of us are born with deficiencies and defects. That does not make us less human or less worthy of respect. Nor should we mandate that defects and deficiencies provide the new standard of behavior for the entire world. When someone is born deaf, do we tell the rest of the world they can never speak or listen to music because it might offend the deaf? Yet that is precisely what transgender activists and the rest of the woke world are trying to impose on our entire society.

"Tell us your pronouns!" "Don't use the term 'mom' anymore. It's 'birthing person.'" "Men can get pregnant," and similar nonsense. The entire world must act deluded because a small number of people truly are. This only fuels the delusion.

5. There is No Basis for Transgender Rights

We seem to be inventing new "rights" in America every ten minutes. But where do rights come from? They can't come from government because a right is something you

108 During the Q&A following my presentation on "Why You Should Not Blindly Follow Your Heart," a persistent biology student at LSU cited the existence of intersexed people to support transgenderism. You can see our widely-viewed exchange on the "Cross Examined" YouTube channel here: www.youtube.com/watch?v=cRPjY-YyHSE&t=227s.

have regardless of what anyone else says about it (including your government). Rights can only come from God (see more about this in the earlier chapter of this book titled "On the Wrong Side of History").

What evidence do we have that God wants anyone to amputate perfectly healthy sex organs? There is none from natural law, the Bible, or any other supposed revelation that claims to come from God.[109]

People can demand that their government legislate or declare certain behaviors as "rights," but that doesn't make them rights any more than a government can legislate that a biological man is a woman. That doesn't make him a woman. Instead of trying to change reality to fit our thoughts, shouldn't we try to change our thoughts to fit reality?[110]

The Health Hazards of Transitioning: What the Media Does Not Tell You

Transgender advocates insist that we ignore biological sex whenever people claim they are a different gender. What someone thinks is all that matters. And they want everyone to bow to that idea either through social pressure or the force of law.

---

109 I think there is good evidence that the Bible is the true written revelation of God (see *I Don't Have Enough Faith to be an Atheist* for that evidence). But even if we judge by the more general natural law standard that founded our nation, we still would not conclude that transgenderism is a right.

110 The difference between those two approaches is the difference between the Left and the Right. The Left wants to change reality to fit their thoughts, whereas the Right wants to change their thoughts to fit reality.

However well intended, that idea is disastrous. When we ignore biological sex to cater to feelings, we not only hurt the health and welfare of the individual but also all of civilization.

At the societal level, we cannot procreate or nurture the next generation by sterilizing people or pumping them with cross-sex hormones. Pretending that men and women can transition and that men can have babies does not make it so. Facts don't care about your feelings.[111] And facts don't yield to your feelings either.

On the individual level, cross-sex hormones and sex reassignment surgeries create health problems that include loss of bone density, increase in heart attacks, breast cancer, diabetes and stroke, and loss of fertility.[112] In fact, a study published by Duke University Press found that trans people die at a rate twice that of non-trans people over any given period.[113]

Some of these negative health effects are partially due to the process of transition, which is extremely strenuous on the mind and body. Complications abound. Scott Newgent, who went through multiple surgeries attempting to transition from female to male, wrote this about the experience:

---

111 See Ben Shapiro's book by the same title.

112 See CJM de Blok, CM Wiepjes, NM Nota, M. den Heijer, Hormoonbehandeling bij transgenderpersonen [Hormone treatment of transgender people: Long-term health effects and safety]. Ned Tijdschr Geneeskd. 2020 Jul 23;164:D4481. Dutch. PMID: 32757514. See also several studies under the heading "Health risks of medical and surgical affirmation" at: segm.org/studies.

113 Landon D. Hughes, Wesley M. King, Kristi E. Gamarel, Arline T. Geronimus, Orestis A. Panagiotou, Jaclyn M.W. Hughto; "Differences in All-Cause Mortality Among Transgender and Non-Transgender People Enrolled in Private Insurance," *Demography* (1 June 2022); 59 (3): 1023–1043. doi: doi.org/10.1215/00703370-9942002.

During my own transition, I had seven surgeries. I also had a massive pulmonary embolism, a helicopter life-flight ride, an emergency ambulance ride, a stress-induced heart attack, sepsis, a 17-month recurring infection due to using the wrong skin during a (failed) phalloplasty, 16 rounds of antibiotics, three weeks of daily IV antibiotics, the loss of all my hair, (only partially successful) arm reconstructive surgery, permanent lung and heart damage, a cut bladder, insomnia-induced hallucinations—oh, and frequent loss of consciousness due to pain from the hair on the inside of my urethra. All this led to a form of PTSD that made me a prisoner in my apartment for a year. Between me and my insurance company, medical expenses exceeded $900,000.[114]

In another article titled, "I Underwent Gender Transition Surgery: Here's What the Media Doesn't Tell You," Newgent went on to describe how doctors and pharmaceutical companies are getting rich by prescribing hormones and conducting experimental surgeries on confused and vulnerable people:

The happy, lighthearted salesmanship of "medical transition" and its blunt reality don't match up. Doctors and medical transition proponents don't prepare you for transition-related post-traumatic stress disorders; they don't mention post-traumatic stress disorder (PTSD) or any of the multiple hardships because it is considered transphobic. I want to tell my story so that others can hear what the medical industry is too afraid to say out

114 Scott Newgent, "Forget What Gender Activists Say. This Is Medical Transition," Quillette (October 9, 2020).

loud: That gender transition surgery is not the magical solution that doctors, the media, and culture describe.[115]

And dare I mention the obvious here, that every new "transgender" patient represents a lifetime of hormone therapy and other related treatments. Nobody has ever "transitioned" (past tense). It is a lifelong commitment of artificially forcing a body to conform to another sex. Cha-ching!

Notice in Scott's description that the medical industry can get away with this because no one wants to be called "transphobic"—heaven forbid! Apparently, it is better to take the money and watch your patients suffer from futile treatments than to risk being called a name.

As we all know (and we don't need studies to know this), it is impossible to change your sex. Pretending otherwise leads to horrific side effects, such as those experienced by Scott Newgent and many others.

When doctors practice medicine properly, they treat males and females differently because that's reality.[116] Yet, too many doctors and counselors are now pretending that the thousands of differences between men and women can

115 Transman Scott Newgent, "Scott Newgent-Underwent Gender Trans Surgery: Here's What The Media Doesn't Tell You," *TReVoices.org* (July 26, 2022): www.trevoices.org/post/scott-newgent-underwent-gender-trans-surgery-here-s-what-the-media-doesn-t-tell-you-dailywire.

116 Ngun TC, Ghahramani N, Sánchez FJ, Bocklandt S, Vilain E. The genetics of sex differences in brain and behavior. Front Neuroendocrinol. 2011 Apr;32(2):227-46. doi: 10.1016/j.yfrne.2010.10.001. Epub 2010 Oct 15. PMID: 20951723; PMCID: PMC3030621: www.ncbi.nlm.nih.gov/pmc/articles/PMC3030621. This paper was published in 2011 before the onslaught of woke ideology that tends to dissuade papers like this (those that affirm differences between men and women) from being published. The paper discusses gender identity and transgenderism, concluding that more study is necessary to see if there are any biological causes for a person's perceived gender identity. To date, none have been found.

be overcome with drugs and surgery. Others are even adopting the political idea that we shouldn't pay attention to biological sex at all.

A case in point is the University of Minnesota medical school. In fall 2022, the school insisted that their incoming class of students take an overtly political rather than medical oath which included recognizing "inequities built by past and present traumas rooted in white supremacy, colonialism, the gender binary, ableism, and all forms of oppression."[117]

Excuse me, but recognizing that there is a true "gender binary" is medically necessary for properly treating patients. Men do not need pap smears, and women do not need prostate checks. Men and women are also susceptible to different conditions and diseases. They also metabolize some medicines differently. Ignoring this can be deadly.

The woke oath also required students to "pledge to honor all Indigenous ways of healing that have been historically marginalized by Western medicine." *ALL* Indigenous ways? If so, this means your future doctors from this school have pledged to consider a "healing dance" on par with proven cures we've discovered through the scientific method![118]

To ask students to take an oath that disregards medical and scientific facts in the name of woke ideology is medical

117 Rexing, Luke. "A Medical Oath: For Science or Social Justice," *The Minnesota Republic* (October 19, 2022): mnrepublic.com/8405/news/a-medical-oath-for-science-or-social-justice.

118 For Native American healing practices, see Koithan M, Farrell C. Indigenous Native American Healing Traditions. J Nurse Pract. (2010 Jun 1) 6(6):477-478. doi: 10.1016/j.nurpra.2010.03.016. PMID: 20689671; PMCID: PMC2913884.

malpractice and threatens the health and lives of everyone. It invites disease and death and is completely counterproductive to the Hippocratic oath. Such "political medicine" is pretend medicine. They are playing with human lives by treating biological facts as mere preferences. People's lives are being destroyed by this political game, including the very young, as we will soon see.

Suicide and Gender Dysphoria

Few want to talk or think about suicide, but it's a tragic reality among teenagers with gender dysphoria and other mental health conditions. Two Harvard Law School graduates compiled data which showed how different mental conditions increase the youth suicide rate.[119] They found that:

- Anorexia increases risk by a factor of 18 to 31.
- Depression multiplies it by a factor of 20.
- Autism raises the risk by a factor of 8.
- Being trans-identified increases suicide risk by a factor of 13.

Well-meaning activists like to suggest that those with gender dysphoria are driven to suicide by social disapproval. Therefore, anyone who expresses anything less than outright celebration for trans ideology and transition is contributing to the problem. If you in any way oppose transgenderism, you will have blood on your hands. Even poor, desperate parents have been met with what can only be described

119 Jane W. Robbins, Esq. and Vernadette R. Broyles, Esq., "The Myth About Suicide and Gender Dysphoric Children:" acpeds.org/assets/for-GID-page-1-The-Myth-About-Suicide-and-Gender-Dysphoric-Children-handout.pdf.

as emotional blackmail from psychiatrists and counselors saying, "You can have a dead daughter or a living son." The same has been said to those opposing anything LGBTQ.

Certainly, social disapproval or *approval* can affect one's state of mind, as appears to be the case with the transgender craze itself. But if social disapproval is the driving force behind trans suicides, then why have there not been similar suicide rates in minority groups that were treated as bad or worse? Dr. Michael Brown observes that blacks were treated much more horribly in this country than gays or transgendered people have ever been. Yet, during slavery and Jim Crow, there was no epidemic of black suicide, nor were black leaders claiming that slavery or racism led to suicide.[120] Moreover, in communities and countries that celebrate all things LGBTQ, the trans and gay suicide rates are still higher than heterosexuals.

Clearly there must be factors other than social disapproval for these higher suicide rates. Look again at the above suicide stats. Notice the other conditions listed—anorexia, depression, and autism—are all mental health conditions. Could it be that mental health is a bigger factor driving trans suicide than social disapproval?

Dr. Lisa Littman's research study found that sixty-three percent of young people had preexisting mental conditions *before* announcing they were transgender. Moreover, almost half had self-harmed, and fifty percent had suffered a traumatic event in their lives such as their parents divorcing,

120 See discussion in Brown, Michael L., *Can You Be Gay and Christian?: Responding With Love and Truth to Questions About Homosexuality Kindle Edition* (Charisma House), p. 19.

being bullied, or suffering sexual abuse.[121] Those factors are already known influences in suicide rates, regardless of any "trans-stigma."

Again, this trauma happened *before* they claimed to be transgender. So, identifying as transgender did not lead to mental health issues; mental health issues led to identifying as transgender.

In many cases, childhood trauma produced the mental health issues which led to the person identifying as trans. That is what Walt Heyer, a former transgender, found. Heyer lived for eight years as a trans woman and later detransitioned to affirm his biological sex before leading the website sexchangeregret.com. Heyer now provides resources to help people detransition. According to one hundred international medical studies, up to twenty percent want to detransition.[122] Heyer said childhood traumatic events triggered him to want to leave his biological sex, which he found true of many people who contacted him.

Heyer has asked thousands of trans people who reached out to him, "When did you (or your child) first feel (or express) gender discomfort?" "What was happening in your life up to that time?" and "Why do you want to destroy who you are?" He said, "One hundred percent of the people have been able to pinpoint exactly what happened to trigger the urge to escape into an alternate gender identity. Their

---

121 L. Littman (2018) "Parent reports of adolescents and young adults perceived to show signs of a rapid onset of gender dysphoria," PLoS ONE 13(8): e0202330: doi.org/10.1371/journal.pone.0202330.

122 See, "Regret is Not Rare," at sexchangeregret.com/regret-is-not-rare.

childhood events run the gamut of abuse, abandonment, and neglect. *Something* always happened."[123]

According to the CDC, these Adverse Childhood Experiences (ACEs) can lead to several health problems down the road. "Toxic stress from ACEs can change brain development and affect how the body responds to stress. ACEs are linked to chronic health problems, mental illness, and substance misuse in adulthood."[124] Heyer writes:

> *When a boy says he identifies as a girl because "I have a female brain," perhaps it's not because he has a female brain but that his brain development has been affected by adverse childhood experiences. This is very common among those with gender dysphoria . . . Thousands of people have written to me and can pinpoint when they first wanted to escape into an alternate identity. The timing often coincides with the ACE. For example, boys who were sexually abused may have an impulse to rid themselves of their genitalia that commenced with the abuse.*[125]

The bottom line is that mental health issues, often produced by childhood trauma, appear to be at the root of dissatisfaction with one's biological sex. It's medical malpractice to dismiss that possibility and jump right to hormones and surgeries. That approach often causes doctors

123 Walt Heyer, "Therapists Treat Dysphoria As A Trauma Symptom, Until It's About Sex," *The Federalist*, (February 17,2022): thefederalist.com/2022/02/17/therapists-treat-dysphoria-as-a-trauma-symptom-until-its-about-sex.
For many resources related to transgenderism, visit: sexchangeregret.com.

124 See Centers for Disease Control, "Adverse Childhood Experiences (ACEs): Preventing early trauma to improve adult heath:" www.cdc.gov/vitalsigns/aces/index.html.

125 Ibid., Heyer.

to miss the underlying factor. This means they are treating the symptoms while ignoring the cause, and that is bad medicine.

Thus, the main factor in trans suicide does not appear to be social disapproval but poor mental health typically triggered by childhood trauma. In fact, ninety percent or more of all people who die by suicide had at least one mental health condition.[126] A politicized medical establishment now only makes matters worse by ruling that diagnosis out of bounds and immediately prescribing cross-sex hormones and surgery.

This does not mean that social disapproval has no effect. That is why speaking the truth on this issue, like all issues of great personal consequence, should be done with great care. We are all made in the image of God and should therefore be treated with respect. Attitudes of condemnation, insults, and bullying are never right and only contribute to a person's fragile mental state. It is not their fault they were traumatized. People identifying as trans need friends who will be loving and truthful enough to get them the appropriate help they need.

It also doesn't mean that we all must agree with one another on every moral and political issue. The LGBTQ community doesn't agree with conservatives on most issues. However, conservatives don't claim this is driving them to suicide. Even if they did, that would not mean LGBTQ people should shut up or keep their opinions and insights—especially helpful ones—to themselves.

126 Jane W. Robbins, Esq. and Vernadette R. Broyles, Esq., "The Myth About Suicide and Gender Dysphoric Children:" acpeds.org/assets/for-GID-page-1-The-Myth-About-Suicide-and-Gender-Dysphoric-Children-handout.pdf.

If we attempt to censor or shut people up, as the Left does, we will lose a vital foundational brick in our civilization—the opportunity to learn from one another and make moral and political progress. Most attempts at censorship are implicit claims of omniscience and infallibility. "Shut up because I already know the answer! There is nothing I can learn from you!"

The hard truth is this: If a person is so fragile that a contrary opinion drives them to suicide, it is not the contrary opinion that is the problem but the person's preexisting mental state. They need good mental healthcare, not the censorship of people who may be saying exactly what will help them solve their problem.

Yet, even if social disapproval *was* the main factor in trans suicide, that would not make agreeing with everything LGBTQ the solution. As we will see in the next section, the data shows that transitioning only makes matters worse. People need to follow the evidence where it leads, not where ideology demands.

Transitioning Makes Matters Worse

People who struggle with gender dysphoria are led to believe that transitioning is the solution to their problem. Unfortunately, due to the politicization of this topic, they are being grossly misled.

The American Psychiatric Association explains on one of their "fact sheets" that in 2013 they decided to replace the diagnostic name "gender identity disorder" with "gender dysphoria," because calling it a disorder would have a "stigmatizing effect."[127] Yet look at some of the many conditions the APA still calls disorders:

- Attention-Deficit/Hyperactivity Disorder (ADHD)
- Autism Spectrum Disorder
- Conduct Disorder
- Disruptive Mood Dysregulation Disorder
- Eating Disorders
- Internet Gaming Disorder
- Major Depressive Disorder and the Bereavement Exclusion
- Mild Neurocognitive Disorder
- Obsessive-Compulsive and Related Disorders
- Paraphilic Disorders
- Personality Disorder
- Posttraumatic Stress Disorder
- Sleep-Wake Disorders
- Specific Learning Disorder
- Social Communication Disorder
- Somatic Symptom Disorder
- Substance-Related and Addictive Disorders[128]

Why does the APA have no problem "stigmatizing" these folks, but as soon as a condition is related to sex, they feel compelled to sugarcoat their diagnosis? Is it possible that certain "fact sheets" contain more politics than facts?

This is clearly a case of special treatment due to the politically charged topic of sex. Yet, changing terminology does

127 American Psychiatric Association: www.psychiatry.org/psychiatrists/practice/dsm/educational-resources/dsm-5-fact-sheets.

128 Ibid.

nothing to resolve the underlying reality that gender disorientation is a clinically diagnosable social identity disorder.

Former transgender Walt Heyer describes how this change hurts the very people it was supposed to help:

> *The stated goal in using the term "gender dysphoria" was to reduce stigma of mental illness for the patients (no longer "disordered"), yet still provide a diagnosis code to satisfy the insurance companies. Consequently, in medical settings today, as soon as a patient mentions gender, most pediatricians, psychiatrists, and psychologists immediately diagnose the person with gender dysphoria and put the individual on a direct path to cross-sex hormones and mutilating surgery.*[129]

He goes on to say, "Gone are the days of counseling to explore why the person has feelings of distress. Patients who voluntarily seek counseling for negative childhood experiences discover it is almost impossible to find a psychologist who's willing to help."[130]

Tragically, the APA revision discourages doctors from discovering and treating the childhood trauma, which is the most

---

129 Walt Heyer, "Therapists Treat Dysphoria As A Trauma Symptom, Until It's About Sex," *The Federalist* (February 17,2022): thefederalist.com/2022/02/17/therapists-treat-dysphoria-as-a-trauma-symptom-until-its-about-sex.

For many resources related to transgenderism, visit: sexchangeregret.com.

130 In a direct attack on personal liberty and the personal freedoms enshrined in the first amendment of the U.S. Constitution, some states have even made it illegal to provide counseling to people who *voluntarily* want to address or change their thoughts about their sexual orientation. A more accurate description of this kind of counseling would be "trauma therapy" rather than the pejorative "conversion therapy;" see: therapyroute.com/article/how-trauma-therapy-is-different-by-a-contreras. If you want counseling to affirm any kind of LGBTQ orientation or behavior, that is fine. Just don't ask for help to go in any politically incorrect direction. That will not be tolerated.

likely reason people experience gender dysphoria. Instead, it fast-tracks people to a treatment protocol that does not work—painful surgeries and a lifetime of cross-sex hormones. Surgeons and big pharma love this—follow the money!

One of the most thorough studies of sex-reassigned people ever done shows this approach does not work. In fact, it shows that people regress. Researchers in Sweden tracked 324 people who had sex reassignment surgeries and compared them to a control group for thirty years. Their findings? As former John Hopkins' Psychiatrist Dr. Paul McHugh wrote in *The Wall Street Journal*, "The study revealed that beginning about 10 years after having the surgery, the transgendered began to experience increasing mental difficulties. Most shockingly, their suicide mortality rose almost 20-fold above the comparable non-transgender population."[131]

Now this does not mean there are not exceptions in which people feel better long after surgery, but the aggregate data should give us pause. The bottom line is, on average, transitioning does not prevent suicide or solve mental health problems. In fact, the severely elevated suicide rate is worse after surgery. The real solution is to provide mental healthcare, not surgery or cross-sex hormones.

That is why Dr. McHugh concluded his article this way: "'Sex change' is biologically impossible. People who undergo sex-reassignment surgery do not change from men to women or vice versa. Rather, they become feminized men or masculinized women. Claiming that this is a civil-rights

131 Dr. Paul McHugh, "Transgender Surgery Isn't the Solution: A drastic physical change doesn't address underlying psycho-social troubles," *The Wall Street Journal* (May 13, 2016): www.wsj.com/articles/paul-mchugh-transgender-surgery-isnt-the-solution-1402615120.

matter and encouraging surgical intervention is in reality to collaborate with and promote a mental disorder."[132]

Dr. McHugh makes sense; we should treat mental disorders with psychiatry, not surgery. He is also exposing flaws in transgender ideology, which may be one reason why transgender activists attack him.

Another reason activists attack him is they recoil at being told they have mental disorders. But what if gender dysphoria really *is* a mental disorder as was admitted long before politics took over? It is certainly against nature to think you're in the wrong body. We are not helping people by denying they have a mental disorder.

It's far better to point out that there is no shame in having medical disorders, especially ones we didn't cause. If someone has a kidney or heart disorder, we don't attach a stigma to that, so why do we do this for brain disorders? We should have compassion for people with all medical conditions, whether mental or physical.

We need to tell the truth to people suffering from gender dysphoria. That means recommending treatments that will actually help them, rather than blindly promoting irreversible treatments that don't work, ignore the real problem, and have horrific side effects.

---

132 Ibid., McHugh. One author of the Sweden study, Cecilia Dhejne, objects to this conclusion by Dr. McHugh because she claims there is evidence from her study that better psychological care for transexuals eliminates the suicide problem. Even if true, this is exactly Dr. McHugh's point: gender dysphoria is a mental disorder that should be treated with mental healthcare, not surgery. One wonders if Ms. Dhejne doesn't realize she's proving Dr. McHugh's point. Perhaps she is blindly bowing to political pressure by her failed attempt to discredit aspects of her own study. See interview on the Trans Advocate website here: www.transadvocate.com/fact-check-study-shows-transition-makes-trans-people-suicidal_n_15483.htm.

Scott Newgent, who says she was originally Kellie King, regrets trying to transition but can't go back. "Medical transition is permanent: period!" Scott writes. "Hormones are permanent and come with lasting effects; we have no clue what is going to happen to these young kids taking them for the rest of their lives. We see kids at 19 with the size of a 12-year-old heart limiting their life; we see young adults who have begun to experience early-onset osteoporosis. We are in a strange place where it's considered 'not loving' to tell the truth."[133]

Scott's health and life have been destroyed, and she believes that money is a big part of the push to transition kids:

> *I would not medically transition again. Medical transition has given me permanent heart and lung damage, recurring bacterial infections for life, and a deformed arm. It cut my dating pool by 90% and took years off my lifespan. This decision has cut short the time my future grandkids will have me, if I meet them at all. So, for me, I am past the bull****. I don't have time for it anymore! Medical transitioning is not for kids. It doesn't fix anything, and it's not lifesaving. But convincing people it is sure makes a lot of money for companies and doctors, doesn't it? A lot of this is about the money. We're talking that if transgender identification continues its current exponential growth patterns, more than 20% of the population will be trans in 20 years—and that is a ton of money!*[134]

133 Interview: Scott Newgent, "Gender Dysphoria Alliance," (April 12, 2021): www.genderdysphoriaalliance.com/post/meet-scott-newgent.

134 Ibid.

You would think the U.S. government would be warning people about this. It is not. On the contrary, the Biden administration is fueling the fire.

The Government is Coming for Your Children (I am Not Making This Up!)

Chloe Cole is a California teen who claims she was coerced into transitioning from girl to boy when she was given puberty blockers and testosterone at age thirteen. At age fifteen, both of her breasts were cut off. At this writing, she is eighteen and suing her doctors for conducting, as she puts it, "Nazi-like experiments" on her.[135]

Chloe claims they said her gender dysphoria would never go away and that she had a great risk of suicide unless she transitioned. True to the recipe demanded by transgender activists, the doctors allegedly asked her parents, "Would you rather have a dead daughter or a live son?"

Upon reflection, Chloe now realizes that her story is all too common in her generation. Like many, she was uncomfortable as a girl at the onset of puberty. Her mindset was made worse by spending too much time on social media sites that lauded everything LGBTQ. Chloe later learned she was on the autism spectrum, but only after her body was mutilated. The doctors did not bother to test her for autism until *after* transitioning her. No sense looking for causes

---

135 James Reinl, "'It's like Nazi-era experiments.' Anti-trans poster child Chloe Cole slams the breast-removal op she endured aged 15 and rallies conservatives to protect other vulnerable kids," *Daily Mail* (January 10, 2023): www.dailymail.co.uk/news/article-11619823/Detransitioner-Chloe-Cole-slams-breast-removal-op-endured-aged-15-child-protection-appeal.html. For an in-depth interview with Chloe Cole, see the Jordan Peterson podcast, (January 3, 2023).

when you've been told what the cause and solution *must* be. Just blindly prescribe puberty blockers and top surgery!

Chloe now sees that her dysphoria was the result of preexisting mental challenges which many vulnerable teenagers are experiencing. She said, "Everybody my age I know who's transitioning, or is dysphoric, they're either on the spectrum, or they have some other learning disorder, or they have depression or social anxiety, or they have a history of abuse or sexual assault, neglect, or issues with their family."[136]

Despite all these complications, some schoolteachers are attempting to transition children without parental notification or consent. Children are being used as expendable pawns in a culture war being fought by Leftist adults who think they have a right to irrevocably alter a child's life, regardless of the evidence, the immaturity of the child, or the wishes of the parents. Meanwhile, trans activists are getting medically conservative doctors fired,[137] and big tech is cen soring anyone who disagrees with transgender ideology.[138] I have a question: If "gender-affirming care" is so great, why all the secrecy, bullying, and censorship?

The answer? If they want to advance their ideology, they cannot allow the truth to be told. Sunlight is the best

---

136 Ibid.

137 For one prominent case mentioned by Dr. Jordan Peterson for its egregiousness, see Jesse Singal, "How the Fight Over Transgender Kids Got a Leading Sex Researcher Fired," *The Cut* (February 7, 2016): www.thecut.com/2016/02/fight-over-trans-kids-got-a-researcher-fired.html.

138 Benjamin Weingarten, "The sinister marriage of woke medics, Biden and Big Tech silencing critics of children's gender treatment," *The New York Post* (October 11, 2022): nypost.com/2022/10/11/the-sinister-marriage-of-woke-medics-biden-and-big-tech-silencing-critics-of-childrens-gender-treatment.

disinfectant, and when sunlight exposes the true results of "gender-affirming care," most people will be horrified.

Chloe would like to be a mom someday. However, because her doctors allegedly exploited her by following a political ideology rather than good medicine, she may never have that opportunity. And if the Biden administration has its way, there will be many more children robbed of that opportunity.

On March 30, 2022, President Joe Biden and his administration celebrated "Trans-visibility Day" by selectively referencing the Bible and then issuing a thinly veiled threat to take children away from their parents if they did not agree with "gender-affirming care."

First, the Bible. The President rightly said that transgender people (like all people) deserve respect because they are "made in the image of God," a clear reference to Genesis 1:27. However, Biden conveniently left out the rest of that verse which disagrees with transgender ideology: "male and female He created them." This does not agree with the assertion of multiple genders, or that God, if acknowledged at all, put trans people in the wrong bodies.

But the more problematic announcement about transgenderism came from the President's administration. Two different subgroups in the bowels of the U.S. Department of Health and Human Services issued documents recommending "Gender-Affirming Care" for *children* to include top surgery (either double mastectomies or breast enhancement), bottom surgery (you can imagine what that means), puberty blockers, and gender-affirming hormones.[139]

Referring to this as "care" for children, the documents claim, "There is no scientifically sound research showing negative impacts from providing gender-affirming care."

That statement could not be more misleading because, at the time, there was not much research either way for children. We just started chemically and surgically "transitioning" children about ten minutes ago! In March 2022, we were light on data about its effects on children.

But do we really need studies to know that cutting off perfectly normal sex organs in children is wrong? Do we need studies to know that immature children whose brains are not fully developed should not be given cross-sex hormones and puberty blockers just because someone on social media enticed them? Can someone in the Biden administration be a grownup?

However, if you want studies, there are some new ones. One released in December 2022 found that gender-affirming care did no better than a placebo.[140] Another 2022

---

139 For a summary and links to all of the government documents, see Timothy H.J. Nerozzi, "Biden administration endorses transgender youth sex-change operations, 'top surgery,' hormone therapy, www.foxnews.com/politics/biden-administration-transgender-agenda-youth-sex-change-hormone-therapy," *Fox News* (March 31, 2022).
See also, Rod Dreher, "Democrats: Party Of Child Mutilators & Kidnappers: Biden Administration lays policy groundwork for removing minor children from families for hormones and surgery," (March 31, 2022): www.theamericanconservative.com/transgender-youth-democrats-party-of-child-mutilators-kidnappers.

140 One new study showed that there was no difference between gender-affirming care and a placebo. See Matt Margolis, "Study: ''Gender-affirming Care' for Children Has No Medical Benefits," *PJ Media* (December 28,2022): pjmedia.com/news-and-politics/matt-margolis/2022/12/28/study-gender-affirming-care-for-children-has-no-medical-benefits-n1656851.

report concluded, "increasing minors' access to cross-sex interventions is associated with a significant *increase* in the adolescent suicide rate."[141]

Meanwhile, "progressive" Europe has seen even more horror stories on their side of the pond. As a result, they are becoming far more conservative on "gender-affirming care" than the U.S. Even the most liberal countries have banned this until a person is at least sixteen or eighteen.[142] They are even closing their gender clinics because of the negative health effects they are seeing. "Not safe" for kids, said a report about one clinic in the U.K.[143] The folks at that clinic have thankfully pledged to shift their focus from hormones and surgeries to mental healthcare.

The danger of child gender clinics is now being acknowledged in America. Jamie Reed, a self-identified queer woman married to a trans man who worked at The Washington University Transgender Center at St. Louis Children's Hospital, had seen enough of the horrific outcomes of so-called child transition. She blew the whistle on her own clinic and left because of the unethical practices she witnessed.

---

141 Jay Greene, "Puberty Blockers, Cross Sex Hormones, and Youth Suicide" *Backgrounder*, 3712 (June 13, 2022). See Jay Greene, "Does 'Gender-Affirming Care' for Trans Kids Actually Prevent Suicide? Here's What the Data Say," The Heritage Foundation (June 15, 2022). www.heritage.org/gender/commentary/does-gender-affirming-care-trans-kids-actually-prevent-suicide-heres-what-the.

142 Dr. Stanley Goldfarb and Dr. Miriam Grossman, "Even progressive Europe won't go as far as America in child transgender treatments," *The New York Post* (January 30, 2023): nypost.com/2023/01/30/even-progressive-europe-wont-go-as-far-as-america-in-child-transgender-treatments.

143 See John Ely and Laurence Dollimore, "NHS will SHUT its controversial Tavistock transgender clinic for children after damning report warned it was 'not safe,'" *Daily Mail* (July 28, 2022): hwww.dailymail.co.uk/news/article-11057813/Controversial-Tavistock-gender-clinic-children-shut-damning-report.html.
See also Matt Margolis, "Sweden Ditches Barbaric 'Gender-Affirming' Care for Kids," *PJ Media* (December 27, 2022). pjmedia.com/news-and-politics/matt-margolis/2022/12/27/sweden-ditches-barbaric-gender-affirming-care-for-kids-n1656568.

At this writing, the Attorney General of Missouri is now investigating.[144]

While the data on children is only now becoming available, we do have extensive data on the effects of transition on adults. As we have seen, there are serious health problems that adults experience from transition treatments, including a loss of fertility. So, don't you think we should hit the pause button on experimenting with children? At least adults can give their informed consent; children cannot.

Now, here's the most sinister part of The Biden administration's plan. It's revealed in the rest of this quote from the HHS text:

> *There is no scientifically sound research showing negative impacts from providing gender-affirming care. The decision for the child welfare system to become involved in the lives of families, potentially to the extent of removing children from their families and homes, should be wielded with the utmost care, grounded in evidence, and always prioritizing the well-being of children and preservation of families.*

Did you get that? They are threatening to take your confused little boys and girls—as young as three—away from you if you do not affirm them as trans and help them transition![145]

144 The Post Editorial Board, "End the Horrors of the Pediatric Gender-Industrial Complex, Now," *The New York Post* (February 12, 2023). See also, Lee Brown, "Missouri AG officially probing 'disturbing' whistleblower claim that transgender clinic 'harming hundreds' of kids", *The New York Post* (February 10, 2023).

145 One HHS document says, "Many children are aware of their own gender identity as early as 3-5 years old, although it is also common for children to explore gender identity at later ages.

As author Rod Dreher put it, "That [HHS statement] ought to send a chill down everyone's spine. **The Biden Administration is laying the policy groundwork for the seizing of minor children from parents, for the sake of jacking those children up with hormones, and mutilating their bodies with surgery!**"[146]

Will we allow this to happen without saying a word? Sir Edmund Burke is attributed with saying, "The only thing necessary for evil to prevail is for good people to do nothing."

Will we allow evil to prevail? How can we call ourselves loving if we do nothing while children are being mutilated before our eyes? If we do nothing, what does that say about us? It says we are neither courageous nor loving. We are cowards who deserve what we allow. Tragically, our children will pay the price for our cowardice.

I know some people are tempted to say, "Look, I'm just one person, what can I accomplish?"

Actually, quite a bit. There are many things you can do to restore our culture to sanity and inform and protect people in your circle of influence. You can pray, read, speak, write, post, volunteer, teach, counsel, vote, and run for office yourself among a thousand other things. And since

---

Cisgender children are trusted to know and understand their gender, and social norms and customs validate their identities regularly. TGI youth deserve the same trust and validation. As parents, caregivers, and providers, *you are responsible to communicate this validation by actively affirming their identities.*" See: www.nctsn.org/sites/default/files/resources/fact-sheet/gender-affirming-care-is-trauma-informed-care.pdf.

146 Rod Dreher, "Democrats: Party Of Child Mutilators & Kidnappers: Biden Administration lays policy groundwork for removing minor children from families for hormones and surgery," (March 31, 2022): www.theamericanconservative.com/transgender-youth-democrats-party-of-child-mutilators-kidnappers.

you're never going to be more than one person, you might as well get started now. In fact, every accomplishment in history—for good or evil—has been achieved by individual persons working toward a goal.

When cultural trends and political tides turn against what is good, true, and beautiful, I pray that you and I will faithfully go in the other direction to fight evil and serve others by doing good. Let's do what's right and leave the results to God. No regrets.

EXECUTIVE SUMMARY

Same-sex marriage is a very emotional issue for many people. However, when one separates emotions from facts, it is clear that the state has compelling reasons to endorse natural marriage and not same-sex marriage or civil unions.

1. Natural marriage is the immune system of civilization. When our marriages are strong, our civilization is strong; when they are weak, individuals and communities suffer.
2. Legal endorsement of same-sex marriage would destroy the institution of marriage, resulting in negative effects on children, crime rates, health and health-care costs, tax rates, and religious freedom.
3. Same-sex marriage activists want to redefine marriage as simply a personal relationship between two committed parties, but marriage is much larger than the two parties involved in a marriage.
   a. Marriage is a social institution of long-established rules (based on the natural design of the human body) that provides society with *the* very foundation of civilization—the procreating family unit. That is, marriage is fundamentally

about children and the civilization of society both now and for the future.

b. Only natural marriage can procreate and consistently provide a nurturing and stable environment for the growth and maturation of children. In this sense, the most basic and effective "form of government" is the natural two-parent family.

c. Statistically, children and adults inside of natural marriage are much better off socially, physically, financially, mentally, and emotionally than those outside of natural marriage.

d. Those outside of natural marriage are not only worse off personally by those measures, but they cost society billions of dollars in social welfare and law-enforcement expenses.

4. The law is a great teacher—it encourages or discourages behavior.

5. Since the law is a great teacher, government-backed same-sex marriage or civil unions would put society's stamp of approval on same-sex relationships and behavior. This endorsement would fundamentally change the institution of marriage to our detriment. It would do the following:

   a. Equate same-sex marriage with natural marriage, thereby teaching citizens the socially disastrous ideas that natural marriage is no better than any other relationship and that marriage is not a prerequisite for children.

b. Disconnect marriage from childbearing by making marriage just about coupling. This will result in soaring cohabitation and illegitimacy and painful costs to children and society.

c. Encourage more homosexual behavior, which is medically destructive to those who engage in it and financially burdensome to the public in general.

d. Result in higher medical, health insurance, and tax costs to the general public.

e. Provide legal grounds to restrict or prohibit religious freedom and free speech.

6. Much of this is already happening in countries that have government-backed same-sex marriage. Natural marriage is weakest and illegitimacy strongest where same-sex marriage is legal.

7. Most homosexuals are not interested in marriage—approximately 96 percent of homosexuals in countries with same-sex marriage *do not get married.* They want *government-backed* same-sex marriage because it would validate and normalize homosexuality throughout society. (Homosexuals can already marry privately and many of them do—what they want is government endorsement.)

8. Some homosexual activists admit that they would like to destroy natural marriage by legalizing same-sex marriage. Since they refuse to live by society's standards, they will only feel validated if they beat down those standards to the level of their own

behavior. If they succeed, everyone in our country will be harmed in some way.

9. All common objections—including those that cite "discrimination" or "equal rights"—are fallacious (see "Answering Objections" below).

How Same-Sex Marriage Will Hurt Marriage, Children, and the Country

Higher cohabitation and illegitimacy rates will hurt children, increase crime, and result in higher costs to individuals and government. Taxes will rise and/or benefits and services will be cut.

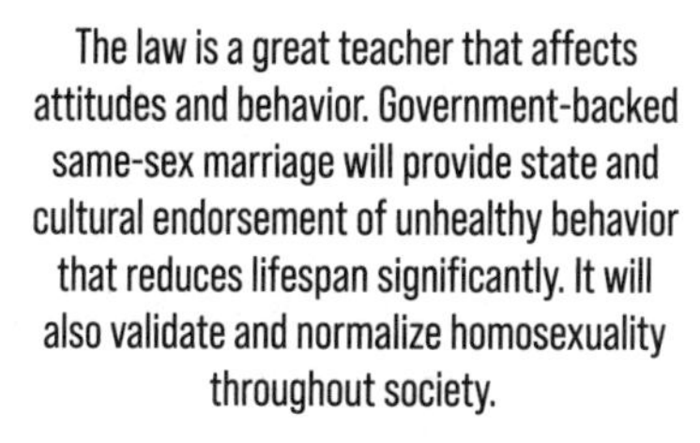
The law is a great teacher that affects attitudes and behavior. Government-backed same-sex marriage will provide state and cultural endorsement of unhealthy behavior that reduces lifespan significantly. It will also validate and normalize homosexuality throughout society.

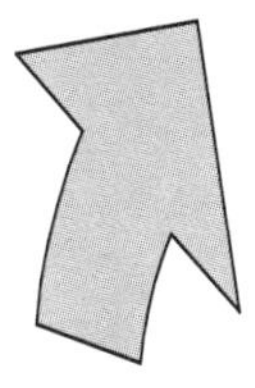

With marriage not culturally necessary for having children, cohabitation and illegitimacy will rise to historic highs (as seen in countries already with same-sex marriage).

Endorsement will likely lead to more homosexual behavior, higher medical and health insurance costs, and restrictions on free speech and religious liberty (as seen in countries already with same-sex marriage).

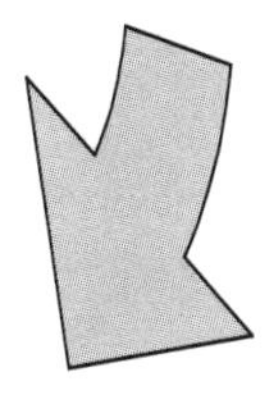

With same-sex and natural marriage equated, marriage itself will become just about coupling; it will not be culturally necessary for having children.

Endorsement will change the institution of marriage by making same-sex marriage the legal and cultural equivalent of natural marriage.

ANSWERING OBJECTIONS

1. **What about equal rights?**

   a. Homosexuals can "marry" one another already—they can pledge fidelity to one another in private ceremonies and do so all the time. But they don't have a "right" to have their relationships endorsed by the state.

   b. Everyone is playing by the same rules: We all have the same right to marry the opposite sex and have the government recognize it, but homosexuals don't like their choices and thus want special rights.

   c. If we grant special rights for homosexuals, on what grounds can we deny special rights for consenting adults who desire other socially destructive or unhealthy relationships such as polygamy or incest?

2. **Don't put discrimination in the Constitution.**

   a. Too late—it's already there. In fact, all laws discriminate, but it's discrimination against *behaviors* not persons; and it's with cause, not arbitrary. For example:

i. The First Amendment discriminates against some Muslims who want to impose their religion on us (a behavior), but it does not discriminate against Muslims as persons.

ii. The Thirteenth Amendment discriminates against businessmen taking slaves (a behavior), but not businessmen as persons.

b. Likewise, current marriage laws discriminate against the behaviors of homosexuals, polygamists, bigamists, adulterers, and the incestuous among us, but they do not discriminate against them as persons.

c. Laws must protect citizens from harmful behaviors regardless of why people commit those behaviors (i.e. sexual feelings do not excuse harmful sexual behavior).

3. But homosexuals are a minority class like blacks.

a. Homosexuals are not a class of people, and neither are heterosexuals. We are males and females, not homosexuals or heterosexuals.

b. You will find many former homosexuals. You will never find a former African-American.

c. Committing homosexual acts is not the same as skin color or gender. Homosexual behavior is harmful; skin color or gender is not. Sexual behavior is always chosen (even if the desires are not).

d. This issue is not about discriminating against people but against the potentially harmful behaviors of people. All laws discriminate against behavior (see #2 above).

4. **But homosexuals were born that way.**

   a. This is an argument from design that backfires because homosexuals were also designed ("born") as males or females. So why should they follow their desires but not the design of their bodies? Failing to follow your desires can be uncomfortable, but failing to follow the design of your body can be fatal.

   b. The source of homosexual desires has not been determined. But even if there is a genetic component (although one wonders how it is passed on because homosexuals don't reproduce), those desires do not excuse behavior.

   c. An orientation toward homosexuality doesn't make the behavior morally right any more than an orientation toward children makes pedophilia morally right. Does an orientation toward violence make gay-bashing okay?

   d. We were all born with an orientation toward bad behavior. Desires, whatever their source, do not excuse behavior. *Should human beings act on every desire they have? Of course not. In fact, the principled restraint of destructive desires is called civilization!*

5. **Weren't you born a heterosexual?**

   a. No, I was born a male.

b. My sexual behavior is chosen just like yours.

6. But homosexuals can't change.

a. Thousands have changed their orientation by their own admission, and studies conducted by a champion of gay activists, Dr. Robert Spitzer, confirm it. Even if they cannot change their orientation, they can, like all people, control their sexual behavior.

b. Why do we expect pedophiles, adulterers, and gay bashers to control themselves but not homosexuals?

7. But some animals engage in homosexual behavior.

a. Yes, some animals engage in homosexual behavior on occasion, but some animals eat their young too. Should we do that as well?

b. When homosexual activists extol animals as their moral examples, what does that say about their own behavior?

8. Opposing same-sex marriage is like opposing interracial marriage.

a. No, ethnicity is irrelevant to coupling; gender is essential. (There is only one race—the human race—but there are two genders.)

b. Opposition to interracial (inter-ethnic) marriage is without merit. Men and women are designed for one another, so inter-ethnic couplings are helpful.

But homosexual couplings go against the natural design and are therefore harmful.

9. **It is unfair discrimination to prevent same-sex marriage.**

   a. No one is being treated unfairly because everyone is playing by the same rules: We all have the same right to marry the opposite sex.

   b. It is not unfair to define who does and does not qualify as a spouse. When the state refuses to recognize a marriage between a father and daughter or a brother and a sister, it is not discriminating unfairly. It is wisely protecting society by choosing not to sanction an unhealthy and socially destructive relationship—for the same reasons the state should not recognize homosexual relationships.

   c. Marriage, by design, is between an unrelated man and woman. The state should simply recognize the natural design of marriage; it should not redefine marriage.

10. **It is bigotry to prevent same-sex marriage.**

   a. No, it is sound judgment based on the evidence that same-sex marriage would be harmful, while natural marriage is healthy and helpful.

   b. This argument, like others, presupposes a moral standard. (Homosexual activists acknowledge that bigotry violates the moral law—why don't they admit the same with regard to homosexual behavior?)

11. But same-sex marriage is about love.

a. Even if it is, so what? Marriage is state-sanctioned because of its social benefits, not to recognize "love."

b. What is loving about medically dangerous behavior? Love seeks the ultimate good of the loved one. Homosexual behavior does the opposite. It hurts people.

c. Most of our loving relationships are non-sexual, yet we don't recognize them by marriage.

12. There are healthy, long-term, homosexual couples.

a. The data show that they are the exception rather than the rule. Declaring an exception does not prove that no rule exists. To the contrary, exceptions prove the rule.

b. Laws must be based on the rule, not the exceptions. If we based laws on exceptions, we would do the following:

   i. Endorse smoking because some smokers outlive non-smokers;

   ii. Endorse drunk driving because some drunk drivers don't hurt anyone.

13. You say marriage should be connected to procreation, but there are some natural marriages that are childless.

a. Again, they are the exception rather than the rule. But the rule is that no homosexual union can procreate (no exceptions).

b. Childless natural marriages can provide a mom and a dad to adopted children, and some have children from previous relationships.

c. Childless natural marriages still affirm what is generally a procreative relationship.

14. Why are you against same-sex marriage when you have already degraded marriage through divorce?

a. True, we've degraded marriage by liberalizing divorce laws, but that's not an argument for same-sex marriage. In fact, it's an argument against it!

b. The vast social problems from the weakening of marriage through liberalized divorce laws show us how important the law is for the protection of the family and why we should not weaken marriage further by approving same-sex marriage.

c. There is one major difference between same-sex marriage and divorce: While divorce has become acceptable, few believe it is a good thing or want our kids to be taught that it's just as good as marriage. On the other hand, those advocating same-sex marriage want it to be endorsed, celebrated, and taught to our kids.

15. Why should the state endorse natural marriage but not same-sex marriage?

a. Because the state has compelling reasons to endorse natural marriage—natural marriage is our national immune system. It protects us from disease and social costs. When our marriages are strong, our society is strong. When our marriages are weak, we all suffer.

b. Natural marriage:

   i. Improves health and lengthens the life span of the man and the woman.

   ii. Protects women from uncommitted men.

   iii. Lowers welfare costs to society.

   iv. Lowers the crime rate (marriage civilizes men and focuses them on productive pursuits).

   v. Procreates and encourages an adequate replacement birth rate.

c. Children from natural marriage homes are:

   i. Seven times less likely to live in poverty.

   ii. Six times less likely to commit suicide.

   iii. Less than half as likely to commit crime.

   iv. Less than half as likely to become pregnant out of wedlock.

   v. Healthier physically and emotionally when they reach adulthood.

vi. Do better academically and socially.

d. Children from fatherless homes account for:

i. 60 percent of America's rapists.

ii. 63 percent of America's youth suicides.

iii. 70 percent of America's long-term prison inmates.

iv. 70 percent of America's reform school attendees.

v. 71 percent of America's teenage pregnancies.

vi. 71 percent of America's high school dropouts.

vii. 72 percent of America's adolescent murderers.

viii. 85 percent of America's youth prisoners.

ix. 85 percent of America's youth with behavioral disorders.

x. 90 percent of America's runaways.

e. Same-sex marriage will lead to more fatherless homes.

16. But homosexual couples can parent just as well as heterosexual couples.

a. The research shows that, on average, homosexual couples provide a far less safe and stable home for children.

b. Family structure is the most important factor in a child's development, and a mom and dad are proven to comprise the best structure. Any exceptions prove the rule.

c. Homosexual relationships always deny children either a mom or a dad.

d. Moms and dads are not interchangeable to children as homosexuals claim. Men and women each have unique contributions to the well-being of children.

e. When homosexual activists are trying to satisfy their sexual desires, they notice a clear difference between men and women. It is only when it comes to parenting that they say men and women are interchangeable. Homosexuals get what they want sexually, but children must settle for whatever their homosexual "parents" give them. This shows that homosexuals tend to care more about their sexual desires than what's best for children, and it's another reason why their relationships should not be equated to marriage.

17. How could allowing same-sex marriage possibly hurt marriage, children, and society?

There is no neutrality on moral issues. By legalizing same-sex marriage, the state would be approving them and therefore promoting them. Laws help change attitudes and encourage good (or bad) behavior. In other words, the law is a great teacher. Many people believe that whatever is legal is moral and that whatever is illegal is immoral. Same-sex marriage will do the following:

a. Trivialize the importance of marriage, leading to increased Illegitimacy and social costs.

    i. Elevating same-sex unions to the level of natural marriage would further downgrade the perceived importance of marriage in our culture. Marriage will be seen as just about coupling rather than procreation.

    ii. This is the case in Scandinavian countries where illegitimacy is exploding partly because people no longer connect marriage to childbearing.

    iii. International surveys show that far more people think illegitimacy is acceptable in countries that sanction same-sex relationships than those that do not.

    iv. Illegitimacy hurts everyone via increased crime and social welfare costs (not to mention the direct harm to children who are denied either a mom or a dad).

b. Lead to higher medical and health insurance costs.

    i. We would likely see an increase in homosexual behavior following the endorsement of same-sex marriage like we saw a sharp rise in abortion following *Roe vs. Wade*.

    ii. Since homosexual behavior, monogamous or not, has been found to be extremely unhealthy, such a rise would hurt the community through higher medical and health insurance costs (see point 18 below for the health effects of homosexual behavior).

18. But wouldn't same-sex marriage improve the health of homosexuals by encouraging them to enter committed relationships?

a. Homosexual behavior is inherently harmful, monogamous or not. The rectum is a one-way street. Forgive the expression, but the rectum is a sewer. It was designed that way. Labeling its abuse as an act of "love" will not change that fact.

b. Even if monogamy helped improve health, such an effect is unlikely because more than 60 percent of homosexuals in "committed" relationships right now are not monogamous anyway. And homosexuals in committed relationships tend to forgo safer sex practices with their partners because they are "in love" and view such practices as an insult.

c. Rather than the man and woman balancing one another, the pairing of identicals feeds compulsive sexual behavior. Anywhere from 21-43 percent of homosexual men have had several hundred sexual partners.

d. Lesbians have more health problems than heterosexual women.

e. Even if health could be improved, that unlikely possibility does not justify making same-sex marriage the legal equivalent of natural marriage. The unique abilities to procreate and parent children should always keep natural marriage as the only legally and socially-encouraged sexual relationship in our society.

19. How would government-backed same-sex marriage hurt you?

a. Higher medical and insurance premiums

b. Higher taxes to pay for the financial benefits of marriage to homosexuals and the social costs that result from increased illegitimacy (including crime and welfare)

c. Reduction of your employee benefits to pay for those of homosexual couples

d. Workplace indoctrination

e. School indoctrination of your children into the "normalcy" of homosexuality (despite the health concerns and moral objections of parents)

f. Preferential adoption to homosexuals at the expense of heterosexual couples (Children will be treated as trophies!)

g. Places of worship may be forced to hire homosexuals

h. Loss of free speech/religion rights (as is now the case in Sweden and Canada)

i. More intrusive and restrictive government regulation to impose the new politically correct morality on you, your children, and your church

20. How would same-sex marriage hurt homosexuals?

a. Homosexual behavior:

i. Results in numerous health problems to those that practice it, including increases in AIDS, other STDs, colon and rectal cancer, and hepatitis. According to the Center for Disease Control, 82 percent of all known sexually-transmitted AIDS cases are the result of male-to-male sexual contact.

ii. Shortens the life span of homosexuals by up to twenty years. (According to the CDC, smoking on average reduces life span by only seven years. Since we discourage smoking, why are we thinking of endorsing homosexuality?)

b. If same-sex marriage is legalized, the government would move from permitting homosexuality to promoting it. So instead of merely permitting people to destroy themselves, the government would be promoting it. Government exists to prevent harm, not promote it.

21. What evidence do you have that these things will occur?

a. Much of what I have said is already happening in countries with same-sex marriage. In Norway, illegitimacy is up to 50 percent nationwide and 70 percent in the most liberal county. In countries such as Sweden and Canada, free speech and religious expression are restricted if they oppose homosexuality. Some pastors have even been jailed.

b. International surveys show that natural marriage is weakest and illegitimacy strongest wherever same-sex marriage is legal.

c. In fact, much of what I have said is already happening in our country. It will only be accelerated by government-backed same-sex marriage. That's why same-sex marriage proponent Andrew Sullivan has written this: "If nothing else were done at all and gay marriage were legalized, 90 percent of the political work necessary to achieve gay and lesbian equality will have been achieved. It's ultimately the only reform that matters. "Sullivan certainly understands that the law will change attitudes and behavior.

22. You say the law is a great teacher. What would a law affirming same-sex marriage teach?

Here are the **FALSE** ideas that a law creating government-backed same-sex marriage will teach:

a. Homosexual behavior is just as moral and healthy as heterosexual behavior.

b. Same-sex marriage is just as moral and beneficial as natural marriage.

c. Moms and dads offer nothing uniquely beneficial to the care and development of children (homosexual couples always deny children either their mom or dad).

d. Marriage is no longer about procreation, just coupling. Therefore, if you want to have children, there's really no reason to get married.

23. We have to be tolerant.

a. Homosexuals already have tolerance. Now they are demanding endorsement.

b. We are to go beyond tolerance to love. Tolerance of evil is unloving because it allows people to be harmed.

c. Homosexuals are not tolerant. They are trying to impose same-sex marriage and its effects through the courts without the consent of the people.

24. You ought not judge!

a. Then why are you judging me for judging?

b. Jesus never commanded people *not* to judge; He showed them *how* to judge.

c. It is impossible to avoid making judgments. Homosexual activists are making the disastrous judgment that same-sex marriage must be endorsed.

25. The separation of church and state.

a. Morality, not religion, is being legislated, and all laws legislate morality. Even a law that legalized government-backed same-sex marriage would be a legislation of morality.

b. The morality affirming natural marriage is being legislated based on good reason and evidence.

c. Just because many churches are against same-sex marriage doesn't mean we can't have laws against it. Most churches are against murder, rape, and theft too, but we still have laws against those behaviors.

d. If this were a valid objection, we could not legalize government-backed same-sex marriage because there are some churches that actually endorse it.

26. What about civil unions?

a. Changing the name of the relationship does not solve the problem—the state would still be putting its stamp of approval on destructive behavior.

b. It is one thing for a society to *permit* destructive behaviors—it is quite another to pass laws that actually *promote* such behaviors. Government-backed civil unions or same-sex marriage would endorse and promote destructive behavior.

ACKNOWLEDGEMENTS

Special thanks go to several people who reviewed this manuscript (or elements of it) as it slowly grew from an article into a book over several years: Stephanie Turek, Dr. Michael Brown, Melinda Penner, Dr. Mark Pustaver, David Limbaugh, Dr. John Ferrer, and Phoenix Hayes. Their suggestions and encouragement were invaluable. Any remaining mistakes are mine.

MorningStar TV